Activate Your Soul, Manifest Your Dreams!

Debra LightHeart

Debra LightHeart Books are available for order
through Ingram Press Catalogues

This book is a personal memoir, and a work of non-fiction. Many accounts are based on the author's direct experience. Some names have been changed to preserve privacy and some incidents have been modified for the benefit of storytelling. This book also contains stories and information shared in the tradition of oral histories that come down through families. As such, all accounts may not be "historically" accurate, but reflect the memories others have shared about events.

Printed in the United States of America
First Printing: January 2015
Published by Sojourn Publishing, LLC

ISBN: 978-1-62747-110-7
Ebook ISBN: 978-1-62747-111-4

What Readers are Saying about Debra LightHeart's Book -
"Activate Your Soul, Manifest Your Dreams!"

"Walk with Debra LightHeart through her powerful healing journey, which offers inspiration for us all, to find our way home to the Love that is our birthright."

- *JoAnne Dodgson, Ed.D, Santa Fe, New Mexico, Author of 'UnLeashing Love', available at (www.pathwaysforhealing.net)*

"Debra Lightheart's healing journey is the quintessential soul pilgrimage. Sharing her personal voyage through the dark pathways and rising light of her life is a true gift of spirit. Her account awakens our soul's yearnings, and motivates us to explore our dark times as we navigate our own soul's journey. Her courage provides inspiration and support to keep trekking through the most difficult passages of our lives, to experience the place of lightness and enlightenment that she has reached. Debra's story is spellbinding. You won't be able to put the book down!"

- *Françoise Paradis, Ed.D., Hidden Springs, Psychological Services, Saco, Maine (www.hiddensprings.info)*

"This is a book of hope! Debra showed me, the reader, that though one has encountered traumatic life experiences, there are tools to work with and spiritual helpers to seek out who can be of great assistance in healing ourselves. I'm left wanting more! Let me sit by your fire in ceremony, let me hear your chants! Let me read more about your experiences of healing the shamanic way!"

- *Nancy Clark, Artist, Turner, Maine (www.artcollectormaine.com)*

Table of Contents

Acknowledgments

Sojourn Publishing

I wish to acknowledge Tom Bird and Sojourn Publishing for helping me to transform from a writer....to an author! Thank you Tom, for your inspiring writing workshop which helped me believe in myself, and realize I could write a book in days or weeks...not years! Thanks to Rama for your patient support and guidance; to Gwen for your vision and energetic support, and Wren for your administrative and technical assistance.

Thanks to all those "behind the scenes", who helped me shape the book to be the best it could be with your expertise in editing, layout and design.

Family and Friends

Although writing can be a very solitary pursuit, it takes a "village" to not only publish a book, but to support the author through the process. Thank you to Joanne, Françoise, Jeff and Nancy for your preview read and helpful feedback!

I wish to thank those who not only supported and encouraged me through the writing of my first book, but who have also been "cheering me on" in my life for many years. You are those who know me on the inside, who have been witness to my journey. You have stood by me through chapters, if not decades, of my life with love and encouragement. When the ground beneath my feet seemed to be giving way, you were the solid support I could count on, along with Spirit, to keep putting one foot in front of the other. You're the Earth Angels in my life. Thank you from the bottom of my heart!

Dorothy, Essjay, Diana, Solange, Nancy and Jaquelin

With deep gratitude to Fred,
for your love, friendship, generosity and unwavering support.

In Memory of June and Snow

Dedication

Dedicated to all the teachers who were instrumental in the healing, growing, and sharing of my soul's gifts, including the writing of this book. It is my prayer that our combined efforts will serve to help many others on their own journeys of healing and remembering who they truly are as spiritual beings of Light and Love.

With deep gratitude to:

All my teachers and allies in non-ordinary spiritual realms;

The animal and nature spirits who have nurtured me on my journey;

The four-legged ones, the plant kingdoms, the stone nations, the winged ones, the creatures of the water, the reptiles and the creepy crawlies, for sharing their wisdom;

The elements of Air, Fire, Water, and Earth for their magic, power and healing;

The ancient lineages of Healers, Wisdom Keepers, Earth Keepers and Star Keepers;

The Q'ero medicine people of the Andes Mountains of Peru and their ancestors;

The indigenous peoples around the world who have held the vision and the sacred ways for all the people during the time of "The Long Forgetting"... and who are helping us to remember our place in the circle of life;

The Emissaries of Light and Love who protect our planet and our galaxy; who seek to help us awaken and reclaim our Light and our Soul's Purpose;

All my two legged teachers who loved me and challenged me to grow my soul, heal my wounds and step into my power and my destiny;

My parents and ancestors, whose struggles and accomplishments made my life possible.

May the love and blessings you've offered me, reach out through this book and inspire many others to activate the power of their souls, heal their lives and manifest their dreams.

May we leave only the imprint of Love upon the Earth and within the hearts of those we meet on life's journey.

Blessed Be.
Debra LightHeart – November, 2014
Santa Fe, New Mexico

Preface

The power of storytelling is one of our most ancient legacies as human beings. We seek to be known, to connect with others through the sharing of our stories, for they can open doorways to healing, understanding and wisdom. If my stories and life experiences can help inspire or offer useful insights to others on their healing journeys, than the true purpose for sharing them will be realized.

I believe healing is an essential act of power that helps us reclaim not only our individual lives, but the well-being of our planet. When we heal core wounds and patterns of suffering; when we honor ourselves as spiritual beings residing in physical form and reclaim the lost aspects of our souls, we collectively create a paradigm shift within our inner and outer worlds. When we heal ourselves, we help heal the whole.

Within the context of this emerging healed and en-LIGHT-ened human, referred to by some medicine people as *Homo Luminous, ("radiant human", or "human of light"*), we become empowered to co-create a world deeply rooted in compassion, wisdom and love; a place where all creation is once again held in our hearts with awe and gratitude; a world where we recognize the god/goddess within each other again, and where loving kindness and compassion are at the root of our thoughts and actions.

This is the emerging era seen by visionary shamans, ancient lineages of medicine people, and all those seeking to "dream a new world into being." This is "the time to come" which is now in the process of unfolding, one step at a time, one soul at a time, until we reach the tipping point that shifts the whole into a new and much expanded, enlightened consciousness, sourced from Love, instead of fear.

My medicine teachers say we become *Homo Luminous*, by cleansing and developing our luminous rainbow energy body and shifting our center of power from the ego and "will center" to the heart. As we do this, we shift our focus from fear and control, to love and trust. We have more spiritual resources available than ever before to help us heal old wounds and awaken our Rainbow Souls. The Wisdom Keepers tell us, many are making this shift within one lifetime. And many souls are now arriving on Earth already carrying this healed soul light, to assist humanity in shifting its consciousness from darkness and fear to light and love.

Our current direction on Earth is not sustainable. To save ourselves and our planet, we must dream a new dream that benefits the whole, not just a few. We must dust off, heal and reawaken our Rainbow Souls, so they once again radiate the divine essence from which we are created. To make such a leap, we must heal the deeply rooted traumas and soul wounds that have left many caught in patterns of suffering, generation after generation.

Each of us who feels the call, must embark on our own healing journey, much as the mythic heroes of old went forth to "slay dragons" in search of the Holy Grail. The outer search is really the inner quest for spiritual truth and meaning, often buried in the rubble of our human existence, lifetime after lifetime.

The stories and life experiences offered here are from my own personal journey from "victimhood" to healing soul wounds for myself, the larger human family and those I've been blessed to assist on their healing journeys. To succeed in my quest, I needed to break free from all the stories and experiences that shaped my false self and sense of powerlessness. I needed to reclaim my soul's true purpose and destiny for this lifetime and beyond.

We will one day co-create a world where fear, greed, violence, trauma, suffering and plundering of the Earth will exist only in teaching stories; mythic tales told and retold, so humans never again forget who we truly are - spiritual beings, whose greatest power is our capacity to LOVE.

Debra LightHeart
Santa Fe, NM
May, 2014

Introduction

In every life there comes at least one moment when we are offered the opportunity to change direction, make a radical life choice; take a great leap into the unknown. I first had such a chance when I was seven years old. My one word answer to an unexpected question would change the course of several lives, but mostly my own. Doors would open to opportunities and experiences I never could have dreamed of in that moment of declaration. At the time, I had no idea I was also saying a much bigger "Yes!" to a journey my soul had agreed to before I was born.

I had come to reclaim my soul's purpose and power. I had come to heal the core wounds that had left me disempowered lifetime after lifetime. I had committed to making this shift, this leap back to my authentic self, in THIS life time. To activate this process, I would need opportunities that would help me to "wake up" from the victim state of being. I would need experiences so powerful I would have "no choice" but to step into my power by healing wounds that were buried deep in my subconscious and soul memory.

Healing is an act of courage. It can sometimes be a reaction to overwhelming pain that pushes us in directions we might never seek out without severe prompting. True healing is an act of reclaiming our authentic power. It's an inside job, a process of recovering who we truly are. For me, this journey has spanned decades and is an ongoing and ever evolving process of peeling away the layers of illusion; a process of remembering and reclaiming my Self and true soul's purpose.

As my healing journey deepened, and my soul's wisdom became more accessible to me, I was drawn to the medicine ways of indigenous healers, energy medicine and shamanic healing. It was through these pathways I was able to access incredible inner resources and spiritual domains as sources of infinite compassion and wisdom. In the realms of the shamanic journey, I began to experience the true power of the soul, not only to heal, but to transform deeply held beliefs and wounds. Through ceremony and rites, I found new avenues for releasing heavy energies and activating new sources of spiritual wisdom and Grace. It is in these realms of Spirit that I was able to most deeply and permanently heal and reclaim my soul, and express its creative gifts.

Immersion in energy medicine and shamanic healing led me to becoming a healing arts practitioner myself, helping others recover their authentic selves while learning powerful processes for self-healing and empowerment. During this process, I was blessed to receive and learn how to transmit sacred rites, which can be cultivated to awaken our *homo luminous* energy bodies, so we become "the shining ones", the Rainbow Warriors of Light and Love.

We owe an incredible debt of gratitude to the Wisdom Keepers around the world. At great peril and personal sacrifice, they have protected and preserved bodies of wisdom and healing practices until the times of *The Great Awakening*. That time has come, and many sacred teachings and wisdom ways once known to only a few, are now being shared for the good of all. These Seeds of Light are being scattered, and are taking root around the globe.

Before I would be ready to receive and grow these seeds myself, I would journey through a time of forgetting, a time of darkness. Like many before me, I would journey through the "Dark Night of the Soul" before I would find my way Home. Yet every step of the way I was held by something unnamable and much greater then myself. Something powerful inside was leading me through experience after experience to ensure I accomplished my soul's mission.

I was surrounded by infinite wisdom and love, as we all are, yet largely unaware of its presence until I began to heal my soul and hear its song.

A Message from the Emissaries of Light and Love

You are here to grow your soul and remember who you truly are as a divine being; a spark of the Divine Creative Life Force. The same creative force that births the stars and galaxies birthed you! But in "The Long Forgetting" of the human species over thousands of years, you have forgotten your place in the cosmos. You have given over your birthright to a few "chosen ones" who carried their Light and shined it upon you. You gave your power to them, even as they came to teach you how to claim your own Light and Spiritual Grace.

The trials set before you in this life, arise out of your own inner beliefs and misunderstandings of life and past life experiences. Your own soul sets you on a path of learning, growth and wisdom according to the life purpose you set in motion before you were born.

If you are seeking to grow a great soul and gather inner wisdom you will need to develop your "spiritual muscle", just as you must develop physical muscle to run a marathon or climb the highest mountain. There would be no growth in wisdom, inner strength, or in your courage, trust or patience, if there were no "tests" or challenges along the way.

The lessons you call into your life are powerful teaching experiences of discernment. Once your soul has acquired such wisdom, these lessons need not be repeated!

You are a unique being! You have your own individual soul-purpose and heart song. When you trust and follow this inner knowing, you will find peace and joy; you will find "greatness" in all that you do. Do not let fear be your guide! Allow love to show you the way. Trust those impulses that come from deep within your own heart and soul. For here beats the eternal wisdom of your soul, where you will hear your own heart's song....and find the path to living the life you came here to live!

(As shared by The Emissaries of Light and Love through Debra LightHeart - August, 2014)

Not every child is welcomed into this world by parents who want them, or who are capable of loving them. Not every child will be born into a life free of hunger, disease, or war. But, whatever our "origins", these are only part of the great illusion of separation. Our true origins are the celestial realms of Spirit, where Love is eternal, and we are eternally loved. Our physical sojourn as spiritual beings on Earth is a great place of learning and growth for the soul.

Soon, we are immersed in the energies that lead us to forgetting who we truly are; entangled in the traumas and dramas of modern day life on Earth. Yet, within our soul, is a deeply rooted knowing that always seeks to guide us back home to ourselves. Much of our healing will actually be a journey of remembering who we truly are, and why we came here in the first place. - Debra LightHeart

Chapter 1

Family of Origin

*I*n the eyes of my young parents, I was "an accident"; the unwelcomed outcome of their teenage passion, most likely conceived in the back seat of my father's prized '53 Chevy. My mother Betty, and her boyfriend, Harry, dropped out of school in ninth grade. Harry modeled himself after movie legend, James Dean, carefully working his hair into a signature wave with the help of Brill Cream, rolling his pack of cigarettes in the cuff of his t-shirt, and wearing his cool, tough guy persona as tightly as a pair of jeans.

My mother grew up on the poor side of Worcester, Massachusetts. Her parents, grandparents and generations before them had migrated from Canada to New England for the factory jobs. She was petite, with long brown hair, cat green eyes and a tough-as-nails veneer that often comes from the grim realities of poverty, with not much of a future to look forward to, other than the excitement of men like Harry.

When I came along, their world turned upside down.

I have just one memory of my father. I was about eighteen months old. When he came into the room, I was standing in my crib. He never approached, but stood rooted a few feet away, eyeing me warily. As our eyes met, I saw filaments of golden light extending from my eyes to his, and from my heart to his. The moment lasted just a few seconds, but burned in my heart and memory.

I don't know the details of what transpired between my parents that day. I only know I never saw or heard from my father ever again.

To my mother, I was the cause of this devastating turn of events in her life. I was the cause of Harry abandoning her, leaving her to fend for herself and me, and the reason for her overwhelming unhappiness. I can recall no loving touch or kind word from my mother in the months and years that followed; nothing but a simmering anger and resentment that was ready to boil over in my direction at the slightest provocation.

The one salvation was that my grandparents, John and Ida, lived nearby, and from time to time we stayed with them. My mother and I would share the narrow couch, when we had no other place to lay our heads at night. My grandfather's good humor, with his beloved blue parakeet Bobo perched on his shoulder, would make me laugh; and my grandmother's home cooking would fill a belly that otherwise, was often empty.

When I was about three, my mother took up with a man named Al, who my grandfather referred to as "that, fat, lazy Frenchman". What my mother saw in him I have no idea. He was considerably older, and as unattractive as she was pretty. The only things they seemed to have in common were drinking beer, smoking cigarettes, loud fights and sex.

With just my mother's welfare check, and three mouths to feed, Al got the idea, and the rare surge of ambition, to build a small cabin in the nearby town of Sterling. He had friends there who owned a rundown dairy farm, and they would be our closest neighbors. Behind their barn lay a scrub field that snaked under the giant power lines serving greater Worcester. Tucked into the trees along the edge, hidden from view, is where Al decided to build our squatter cabin. For years the farm had used this field as their dump; strewn about were abandoned refrigerators, broken toilets, a beat up black cook stove, and piles of tires.

The cabin was constructed of rough pine boards, and featured two rooms – Al and Betty's bedroom, and an all-purpose room that served as a kitchen, living room and the place I slept in my crib. A woodstove provided a cooking surface and heat; kerosene lamps offered light in the evening, and a bucket behind a tattered stuffed chair served as the indoor toilet. A nearby spring was our source of water carried to the cabin in buckets and jugs. From time to time Al's friends gave us milk and eggs from the farm, or sent us home with fresh baked bread and sweets.

Before long, we had also acquired a menagerie of animals. First there was a collie dog, which turned out to be pregnant and delivered twelve puppies. There was the small grey cat that had six kittens. Then one morning the goat surprised us with her baby kid...who delighted me to the point of hysterics with its stiff legged bounding around the yard. We even had a few hens scratching about. This country life with animals and fresh air suited me. I had a natural affinity for animals and nature, along with boundless curiosity. I could entertain myself for hours lost in the magic and mystery of nature. Barely more than a toddler, and often left unattended, this would prove to be a mixed blessing.

The abandoned appliances made for an engaging playground for a three year old, and baby animals were compliant play mates, including a little white kitten I named Snowball. I found it very entertaining to put her in one of the old toilets and watch her try to climb out and slide back down the porcelain sides. One day after we'd had a big thunderstorm, I ran outside to play our game. But this time after a little while, she stopped trying to climb out, and soon stopped moving at all.

I lifted her wet, lifeless body out of the toilet's rainwater, not realizing I had drowned my kitten. When my mother told me what I had done, I was heartbroken and began to cry. I was sure I'd get a licking too, but this was one time my mother seemed to take pity on me. My sorrow was punishment enough. Shortly thereafter, I was discovered "baking puppies" in the oven. Trouble was, on a hot day, my life size play stove was like a real oven. Fortunately, I was found out in time, and no harm was done. After that, Al set about removing the doors on the abandoned refrigerators for fear I'd hide in one and suffocate.

Living on welfare checks, meant that by the end of the month, times were usually lean, and food nearly gone. One day, a truck arrived unannounced at our door, and two men delivered several boxes with large unmarked cans. That evening, my mother pulled out three bowls and opened two cans of food. She divided the contents equally, setting two bowls down on the floor for the dogs, and putting the third bowl (with a spoon) on the table for me. She stood nearby smoking her cigarette saying, "I'd never eat such disgusting stuff."

I remember feelings flooding through me, a sense of shame and humiliation that in my mind, I was being fed "dog food". I burned with anger, disgust and self-loathing. The feelings, washed over me like a bucket of scalding hot water. Of course, I was too hungry to refuse. So I ate my "dog food", eyes glued to the table, while my mother lit up another cigarette with the glowing embers of the one before.

One day at lunch, I accidently spilt my glass of water. It soaked my piece of white bread, turning it to a soppy paste.

My mother yelled at me, "We can't afford to waste food! You ain't leavin' this table until you eat the mess you made!"

Although Al protested, I was forced to stay and eat the soggy bread, gagging on every bite. Another night not long after, when I reminded my mother we'd not had supper, she shoved a raw potato into my hand to eat, instructing me to, "Stop whining, before I give you something to whine about!"

I was also repeatedly told to, "Stop your runnin'! You'll wear out your shoes! You'll be puttin' us in the Poor House if you don't quit it!"

Well, I didn't "quit it" in my childhood enthusiasm for exploring my outdoor surroundings. But, a few good spankings set me straight. I learned to walk and not run; to sit still and not squirm. Soon, I was a plump little girl, who by the end of the summer still had holes in her cheap shoes, which were now also too small. My mother ignored my complaints until she saw my bloody feet, the nails of my outside baby toes split in two.

Al and Betty would count down the days until the welfare check would come in the mail. On one rare "family" occasion, they decided we'd all walk to town to get an ice cream. When we got to Sterling, Al hoisted me up on his shoulders, and for a little while I felt on top of the world. But more often, the welfare check would be cashed to purchase as much beer as could be carried, along with cigarettes. Food was purchased with what was left.

One day when the check came, my mother announced she and Al were going into town and leaving me at home. She plopped me on her bed like a rag doll, and told me to stay there until they got back. All I remember is the world going black, and the walls closing in around me in my terror of being left all alone. I was three years old. I have no memory of how long I laid there, or what they found upon their return.

Al gave up on the idea of a hand-dug well about six feet down, and soon abandoned his dream of homesteading altogether. Without a car, the walk into town was getting old and there was no way to hold down a job out here. With winter coming on, Al and my mother gave all the animals away except the little grey cat, and we moved back to Worcester. I dreaded our return to the city.

Chapter 2

Holloway Farm

*N*inety miles north and a world away from Worcester lay Holloway Farm. It was one of several small to medium sized dairy farms straddling a stretch of the Souhegan River valley in southern New Hampshire. Lyman Gale had purchased the abandoned house on a hundred acres for the tidy sum of $5,000 as a wedding present for his daughter, June and her second husband, Snow Holloway, in the spring of 1949. For more than a dozen years the Holloways had spent their retirement turning the dilapidated old homestead, fallow fields and sagging outbuildings into a gentleman's farm.

Holloway Farm sprawled across rich, flat river bottom soils nurturing acres of lush pastures and meadows. The property boasted abundant woods, cow pastures and hay fields, high bush blueberries, a bog, and a long stretch of meandering river frontage. The main house, a 1760's center chimney cape which was sinking into the cellar when purchased, had been meticulously restored and updated. The post and beam structure had been secured back on its granite foundation. Old horse hair plaster walls were repaired or replaced. The wainscoting and wide floor boards had been stripped of years of accumulated paint and grime, restoring the original wood luster. The nine over nine window frames had been restored and the old wavy glass reset with fresh putty.

The huge kitchen fireplace, the mainstay of every house of the period, had been rebuilt to hold the long cooking crane, and boasted a double beehive oven. Every room was furnished with museum quality antiques collected over the generations by June's family - Windsor chairs, Sheraton and Chippendale tables, secretary desks and highboy dressers; Canton and Staffordshire china, American and English Pewter, antique clocks, gilded mirrors, Persian rugs, an elaborate silver tea service, colonial whale oil lamps and a large collection of antique tools were assembled in impressive array.

The master bedroom suite addition featured a tile compass inlaid in the floor and double private baths, a feature quite unusual at the time. A large screened porch and outdoor shower were among the amenities to be enjoyed after a busy day on this gentleman's farm. All structures and outbuildings were painted a signature barn red.

Attached to the main house the Holloways had built a large "carriage shed" which housed their Chrysler Imperial and Ford pickup truck, tractor and a stable with three stalls, small tack room and hayloft overhead. Just down the gentle slope of the yard, was a massive dairy barn designed by June Holloway. The gambrel roofed structure featured the most modern amenities available at the time – automatic gutters to clean out behind the cows and go directly into the manure spreader, watering bowls for every cow, glass bricked calving pens and a state of the art milking parlor with electric milking machines. Forty metal stanchions were generously spaced and identified with the name and pedigree of the cows, each one named for a wildflower.

While Snow milked the cows twice a day, June would accompany him on the evening rounds to spread a generous bed of sawdust under each doe-eyed, fawn-colored Jersey. She groomed several cows each evening, attended the birth of the calves in the spring, and sometimes drove the tractor to help bring in the chopped silage for the herd of prize-winning Jerseys.

Snow had strung miles of fencing traversing low and high pastures, built the duck house on the pond, horse stalls and sheep pens, milked morning and evening and tirelessly tended the many farm related chores. During the spring, he would dutifully tow to safety with the tractor, those wayward travelers who ventured down the muddy road overrun by seasonal flooding. In fall, the tractor mounted wood splitter could be heard cracking in the crisp air, a prelude to cozy fires. In winter, he used the front end loader to clear deep snow, making ample passageways for cars and the tanker trucks that came weekly to pick up the farm's milk.

Snow now used the tractor to do much of the work he'd once done with just his pair of black Percheron draft horses, Pete and Repeat. They stood some eighteen hands tall, and had hauled the water wagon at a full gallop to many a fire. Snow had purchased them at auction, bringing them out of retirement for farm work. He sure could mow a field in record time with that pair! Snow missed the old days, and the quiet ways of working his team of horses. But he loved working the farm and being a dairyman again.

When Snow wasn't busy with the multitude of farm chores, he'd retire to his workshop to build by hand his double and three-masted schooner model ships. Hand carving the hull, deck and masts, he'd meticulously craft the rigging, sails and gear, finishing each one with several coats of paint and varnish. From dories to three-masted schooners, boats had helped shaped Snow's boyhood on the mid-coast of Maine. Farming and the sea were what set him free.

June's father built "Pasture House" just up the road from the main homestead after his wife died. He lived on Holloway Farm for the last ten years of his life. He and Snow were constant companions, as the retired investment banker now preferred sneakers and road trips in the farm pickup truck to the boardrooms of Boston. He and Snow would peruse the Weekly Farmer's Market Bulletin, looking for exotic hens or other fowl and set off in Snow's pick up for an excursion. Over time, Guinea Hens, Silkies, Bronze Turkeys, Homing Pigeons and

Muscovy Ducks were among the feathered flocks roosting at Holloway Farm.

Meanwhile, June was tending the books, writing and giving lecture demonstrations of her impressive collection of antiques and antique tools. Her grown daughter, Essjay, and three young grandchildren visited the farm often. June would spend time with the grandchildren while Essjay taught horsemanship classes to local children in the large outdoor arena.

June was very proud of her daughter who had graduated from Tufts University - School of Veterinary Medicine, the only woman in her class. But she was also frustrated that Essjay had not followed her dream (or her mother's dream for her), to become a veterinarian; rather she had married at a young age and started her family with a man June did not entirely approve of. Nevertheless, she was pleased to be surrounded by family at the farm. Her life was satisfying and stimulating.

When her father Lyman died, it marked the end of an era, and a way of life. In the dark days following his death, and the bitter feud that ensued between his three adult children over disbursement of his estate, the glory days of Holloway Farm faded quickly into the past. Snow and June, now in their mid-sixties, no longer had the heart or the energy to keep running Holloway Farm. The question now was; what next?

There may come a time when you believe we have abandoned you. But in truth, it is you who falls asleep, and forgets us. We do not judge you for this, for we see the many veils that fall across your soul as you enter the dense and chaotic energies of your modern world. But we are always with you, gently reminding you to "wake up!" to the beauty and preciousness that you are.

We are your angelic teams and guides. We hold you in our total and complete unconditional love. There is nothing you can say or do that will drive us away from our "soul purpose" of loving you completely, and reminding you again and again, to love yourself and others as we so love you.

Your Light and Your Love are greatly needed on the Earth at this time!

The Emissaries of Love and Light...Through Debra LightHeart 2014

Chapter 3

Nightmares Begin

Our lives in Worcester resumed with new routines as my world slowly faded from color to black and white. The comforting conversations with my angels began to fade and then stopped altogether. When they visited, I had felt completely safe and filled with love. The adults thought I was talking with my "make believe friends", as I had no playmates, and I was content to let them think just that. I seemed to know things the adults didn't, and I learned to keep those things to myself. Nevertheless, the innocence and magic of childhood soon slipped away as I practiced being invisible to not attract the steely attention of my mother.

Betty found work in a factory nearby, and Al returned to his main profession of dump picking, with me riding shotgun. He'd always buy me a sweet or a soda and seemed to enjoy my company. He'd pick through the dump looking for scrap metal, worth the most, or an occasional find that he could resell. He also kept a look out for discarded toys for me.

For my part, I tried to avoid stirring my mother's wrath, and set about being the best behaved little girl and mother's helper. I'd sweep, wash the floors and drag a chair to stand on over to the kitchen sink, so I could wash the dishes. I made my bed, and was sure to return my broken toys from the dump to their cardboard box in the corner.

On a rare outing, a nice cousin of Al's and his wife took me to White City, a local fair ground and park in Worcester. The only ride I requested (three times!) was the merry-go-round on a beautiful painted pony that moved up and down. The couple bought me my first cotton candy, and tickets for games of chance. Bingo! I actually once won a prize…a beautiful, pink ceramic poodle. I couldn't wait to bring it home and give it to my mother. She collected pretty things, and I knew she'd love it. I couldn't remember being so happy.

As we crossed the tarmac on our way to the car, the beautiful treasure slipped thru my fingers, shattering in pieces at my feet. I burst into tears. When we got home, I stood with my head hanging in disappointment as the woman explained what had happened. Her words hung loosely in the air until my mother's reply batted them away.

"She probably did it on purpose," she said glaring at me, then turned on her heel, reaching into the refrigerator for a beer.

Now that my mother was working, the welfare check didn't come. When I got sick with chickenpox, and she missed a couple days work at the factory to stay home with me, she was fired. That afternoon, my mother burst through the door, red faced. She grabbed me by the hair and shoved me into my room and onto my bed against the wall shouting in my face, "I hate you, I hate you, I hate you! " Her words were like knives flying through the air.

I knew I was the cause of my mother's unhappiness and I began to hate myself for it. One day when I was home alone, I opened a kitchen drawer and pulled out a large carving knife. I held it up to my heart, tears streaming down my cheeks, wishing with all my might I could end all our misery by killing myself. I was four years old.

When Thanksgiving came, we had no money, no food and no place to go, until Al told us we were invited by one of his relatives for Thanksgiving dinner. My mother and I made the long walk in the cold. I was so hungry it felt like I'd been punched in the stomach. We finally arrived and knocked on the door. A sour smelling woman with a pinched red face opened the door.

"What the hell do you want?"

"Al told us you'd invited us over for Thanksgiving dinner," my mother replied in a shriveled voice.

The woman spat her words at us, "That lazy son of a bitch! Let him catch his own God damn turkey!"

She slammed the door in our face. We made the long walk home in silence, hunger growling in our empty bellies.

The following spring, on a day I was again accompanying Al on his dump runs, he pulled the car up in front of that same house. He told me to wait in the car while he checked things out. Shortly, the same red faced woman answered the door, casting a snarling look my way. Al beckoned me to come on, and we climbed up the steep, narrow stairs to the dingy living quarters. To my surprise, there was a little girl about my age. Soon we were engrossed in play in the corner at the top of the stairs, paying no attention to the adults' conversation. The little girl had the most beautiful doll I had ever seen. It was over two feet tall, with long hair and blue eyes that closed when she was put down to sleep. She had a wardrobe with clothes, shoes, a brush, and a comb which I was drawing through her long brown locks.

The woman came and stood over us for a few moments, her stained apron and thin cotton dress brushed against my hair. Her grey slippers were split at the front seam and her toe nails poked through like yellow teeth, forming an ugly smile. She stepped back to talk with Al, as I made a few final strokes thru the doll's beautiful hair. I leaned back as I had before, seeking the support of the door behind me. But this time, there was only the rush of air, shock and helplessness as I fell backwards, head over heels down the long, steep, dark wooden stairs, landing in a heap at the front door, still clutching the doll's comb in my tiny hand.

I didn't cry. I knew that that mean woman had unlatched the door deliberately. I wouldn't give her the satisfaction of seeing me cry. Al and I quickly left. The next day I was covered with bruises and had a goose size "egg" on my head. There was no trip to the doctor or comforting by my mother. It was just another one of the knocks of life, and I'd better get used to it. We never visited that relative again.

The summer before I started school, Al found us an abandoned house in the country to spend the summer. He had an odd lot of relatives, and supposedly this place had belonged to a deceased aunt. It was livable downstairs, as the house was still furnished and had running water. It sat on a knoll overlooking a small pond. What I hated was the attic where I slept.

Summer nights were long and hot. I was put to bed while the sun was still up and the room was stifling and smelled of old dead things. In the corner was an active wasp nest. Every night I lay in terror believing that once the wasps discovered me, they would swarm and sting me. Despite my fears and protests, the nest remained. There were mice too. Every night, Al would set a mouse trap under my bed. I'd lay awake waiting for the wasps to swarm, and the trap to snap. Each morning, I'd wake to find a freshly killed mouse beneath my bed and the ominous hum of wasps at work.

As the summer wore on, I began having nightmares of a different kind. A heavy, smothering would come over me so I couldn't breathe. A dark shadowy monster with foul breath that made me want to throw up. I tried to scream, but no sound could come out, as my heart raced in terror. In the morning all would fade, until the next night, when I lay in bed hyper vigilant for all those things waiting for me in the shadows.

I told my mother my nightmare. It was so real. "Someone is coming in my room at night and getting in bed with me! And then I can't breathe!"

"It's just Jiminy Cricket trying to get in bed with you," she replied, not looking up from her ironing.

We had just gone to see the movie Pinocchio. Imagined or real, I knew whoever or whatever was coming to my bed or my dreams at night, was NOT Jiminy Cricket.

Chapter 4

Snow Meader

Snow was born in Topsham, Maine, April 16, 1903 to Horace and Cora McKinney. Cora had fled her mother's home in the dead of winter to elope. She was just nineteen when she gave birth to little Snowie. His sister Annie arrived two years later. Their father worked long hours in the local mills, while their mother struggled to raise two young children largely on her own. She was never of a strong constitution and was often bed ridden for weeks at a time. When the children were just nine and seven years old, she died of tuberculosis. Horace had no emotional or financial resources for raising the children on his own, and no family to help out. And so it was the children's grandmother, Angelia Meader, of Boothbay Harbor, Maine arrived one night, unannounced, and whisked the children away into her stern but loving care.

Angelia was from an old Boothbay family boasting a long line of seafaring men. When her husband, Captain Alonzo Meader died, she remained in their family home, a classic Maine Cape on the hill, overlooking the harbor. Like many houses of the era, the out buildings were attached in a long series of ells leading out to the privy, the wood shed and a small barn. In the harshest of weather, one need never go out into the elements to fetch firewood, or tend the family horse and cow. The five acre property also featured a small orchard and ample space for the large vegetable garden and flower beds Angelia adored.

Like most homes in the neighborhood, hers was painted white with green trim, had a steeply pitched roof to brave the snows of a Maine winter and boasted a front porch with beautifully turned railings. Inside, were wide pine floors worn smooth with age, Angelia's handmade braided rugs and simple, functional furnishings. She heated the house with coal in the parlor stoves, and wood in the great Atlantic cook stove that was the heart of the home.

In her summer kitchen ell, was a smaller cook stove for turning out the many quarts of canned fruits and vegetables from her garden. By fall, the shelves were lined with mason jars brimming with green beans, piccalilli, pickled beets, tomatoes, wild blueberry, plum and pear preserves and jellies. Dried apples, and herbs were strung from the rafters, while in the root cellar, potatoes, carrots and several varieties of squash offered a winter's worth supply for hearty meals. Flour, sugar, lard and spices from the local grocery, filled in the gap, along with fresh fish, lobsters or clams depending on the season. The milkman delivered fresh cream and milk to the back door twice a week and a few hens gave plenty of eggs for a family of three, along with an occasional chicken dinner.

Early 1900's Boothbay Harbor was a bustling community; a temporary safe haven for the dwindling numbers of merchant ships bearing goods from Europe and Asia; and a summer destination for wealthy families from the suburbs of Boston and New York City, escaping the heat and crowds of the big cities, to summer in their "cottages" dotting the inner harbors and rugged coastline. It was home to lobstermen, heading out at dawn to haul and reset their traps, and fishermen who ventured beyond the safety of the harbor to make their living. It was a place alive with the scents of salt air and balsam pine, the play and cry of gulls overhead, and the ever changing mood of the sea lapping at the docks and rocky shores.

For Snow, life in Boothbay Harbor was heaven, and he savored as much of it as he could when not in school, doing chores for his grandmother or fidgeting at church Sunday morning. He'd hang out by the wharves and watch the great ships being off-loaded, and the snappy bidding at the fish auctions for the day's catch. He and Annie would admire the finely dressed summer folks on route, by horse and carriage, to their summer estates; and aimlessly peruse storefronts with their array of goods to dazzle the eye. Children were not welcome in the finer shops and Snow and Annie would soon be shooed out by a shopkeeper brandishing a broom!

The sardine factory was the biggest employer in town, and soon Snow found an enterprising way to earn his first regular income. It was a messy business, as the women prepared and packed the sardines at record speed, seated at long wooden tables. Large tubs overflowing with sardines were delivered like clockwork to keep up the pace of one of the largest canneries in New England. Along with the sardines, other fish were caught, but not suitable for canning, including sunfish and smelt. These glistening fish lay like beautiful coins waiting to be gathered up by an industrious boy. Soon Snow had a regular business, filling his red wagon with cannery fish "throwaways" and selling them door to door up and down the streets of town. On the weekends, he found another more gentile venue for his services, as a portrait model at the summer artist colony up on the hill. Being handsome as well as handy gave Snow a leg up on most anything he set his mind to.

For a treat after chores on Saturdays, Angelia would give Snowie and Annie five cents each to spend at Trask's Country Store. There they would each fill a small striped paper bag with a variety of succulent candy treats - licorice whips, lemon drops, peppermints, horehound, cinnamon bark, all day suckers and more. With a left over penny, Snow would bob for an extra-large pickle from the huge glass pickle jar, and rummage for the accompanying soda crackers in the nearby tin.

Sometimes on a hot summer day, the children squandered their nickel for a summer ice, or they'd help their grandmother by cranking the ice cream maker for what seemed like hours, until their creamy, cold confection was ready to serve. But until then, sharing the lickings on the wooden paddle was reward enough for their efforts. When in season, they would top their home made vanilla ice cream with wild blueberries or strawberries for an extra special treat.

One day, when Snow and Annie were crossing the foot bridge across the harbor, Annie accidently dropped her nickel. It fell thru the slats of the bridge into the shallows below, and lay glimmering amid the seaweed, pebbles and clams. Annie began to cry. While Snow did his best to console her, a passerby asked what was wrong. Upon hearing their tale, the kind lady gave the pair a quarter each! That gave them a brilliant idea. Annie produced tears for several more passersby until they had collected the mighty sum of one dollar! By then, Snow's conscience got the best of him. So they went shopping for an extra treat that day, and put the rest in their secret savings Snow was keeping. But they wouldn't be telling their "Grandma Gar" about the "donations" they'd acquired that day. It would be their secret.

Snow was also earnest about learning trades and skills that would serve him his whole life. By the time he was fifteen, he had set his hand to many a task; helping his aging grandmother tend her large kitchen garden and perennial beds, and neighbor farmers to build fences and mend stonewalls. He learned animal husbandry, from tending horses and cows, to sheep and chickens. The summer he was fourteen, he worked as a blacksmith's assistant aboard a three-masted schooner, preparing for a voyage to Europe. Snow was devastated when his grandmother would not let him accept the captain's offer to be his ship's boy. The Lorna Doone set sail in the spring of 1917. The ship and all her crew were lost at sea, somewhere in the cold, deep Atlantic.

Snows' uncles, like his grandfather Alonzo before them, owned a fleet of fore-and-aft rigged Down-easter merchant ships. These were the sturdy workhorses of the sea, built to ferry heavy loads of timber and granite up and down the coast in fair weather and foul. One of the last of the fleet had been named the Cora Clara for Snow's mother. But the days of merchant ships were coming to an end, along with Snow's dreams to sail across the sea on one of them. So instead, Snow signed on as a stable boy at the livery, and soon was driving wealthy tourists and seasonal summer residents to their elegant homes overlooking Boothbay's rugged coast. With his congenial manner and knowledge of the area, Snow earned generous tips and was rapidly building his savings.

The winter following Snow's sixteenth birthday, his grandmother became ill with pneumonia. Snow ran to town on a bitterly cold night to fetch the doctor. Despite following her doctor's orders and round the clock care by her grandchildren, Angelia died in Snow's arms a few days later. Snow and Annie lay their grandmother on her bed, covering her body with one of her own handmade quilts. They shed their tears of grief and sat with her for the entire afternoon, until the sunset splashed colors of red and pink on the white washed walls and the pine trees cast long shadows across the room.

Two days after the funeral, they were packed up with a few belongings by their Uncle Howard from Massachusetts. They drove to Waltham in silence, Snow feeling the walls closing in as his life and dreams tumbled down around him.

Angelia had died comforted by the knowledge that her home, financial savings and investments would be enough to provide for Snowie and Annie. She had shown Snow where the key was hidden for the large trunk in the living room. She had opened it one day and carefully removed the leather folder containing her will. She read it aloud to Snow. Her two brothers, who were already well established and successful businessmen, were to inherit five dollars each. The rest of her estate was to be divided equally between Snow and Annie when they came of age. A financial guardian would be appointed if needed.

There was one thing Angelia hadn't planned on - her brother Howard's greed. It only took one meeting with a lawyer to undo the will since both children were under age and Howard was next of kin. He became their self-appointed guardian, and trustee of the estate. The house on the hill and most of its contents was sold. Howard pocketed the generous sum as payment for taking in the two waifs. Neither Snow nor Annie ever saw a penny of their inheritance.

Snow seethed with anger and hatred of his uncle from the start. Even his own hard earned years of savings had been usurped. Each time Snow challenged his uncle, he was badly beaten. Finally, he told Annie, he couldn't stand it any longer, as he'd just as soon kill his Uncle Howard as look at him. He promised his sister he'd find work and send her money as soon as he could. Then one night, while everyone lay sleeping, Snow packed up his few belongings and slipped silently out into the cold darkness, suddenly a man at sixteen, penniless and alone.

Sometimes, those closest to us are caught in a deep place of forgetfulness. They may be living with great suffering in their heart and soul and seek to fill their emptiness with a false sense of power. They may be lost in the darkness of a troubled mind and project their darkness upon us, or steal our Light.

As children, we are sponges to the energies around us, and are defenseless against the assaults on our mind, body and spirit. When these energies become too intense, we protect ourselves the best we can, often by disowning and repressing parts of ourselves. While we are never completely separate from Spirit, parts of our soul may leave as a way to protect us from the full brunt of trauma. These parts literally find sanctuary in another dimension.

As a result of losing these quanta of energies, we experience a "hole in the soul" which we seek endlessly to fill, in our unconscious efforts to heal this inner void. The retrieval of these lost (and healed) soul parts, along with their accompanying gifts, is essential for complete healing of trauma and reclaiming our personal and spiritual power.   *- Debra LightHeart*

Chapter 5

The Visitor

$\mathcal{A}$nother "country house" summer was drawing to a close. One evening my mother put me to bed in the crib downstairs. The sun was streaming into the room, and I felt a deep peace and joy filling my being. I lay contentedly in that space between worlds and said aloud, "I love you Mommy."

My mother sprang from her chair, yanked me up by the arm and gave me several hard wallops on my behind yelling, "I told you to go to sleep!" and shoved me back down in the crib. I lay curled up in a ball, and cried myself to sleep.

On our final summer weekend, Al led us down to the pond where a leaky row boat was tied to a tree. We all three clambered aboard, and Al took us on a lazy paddle around the small pond. The sun was dazzlingly bright, bouncing off the water, and bringing tears to my eyes. A light breeze stirred and ruffled the smooth surface. The only sound was our wee boat moving through the water and the rhythmic stroking of the oars. I soaked up the afternoon, letting it warm my memories and spirit. It would have to nourish me for the foreseeable future.

We returned to Worcester and rented an upstairs storefront room with a community bathroom down the hall. I slept on the floor at the foot of Al and my mother's bed. One night I awoke to the sounds of my mother moaning in pain. As the night wore on, she was crying out in agony, asking Al to do something. I lay in anxious fear for the pain my mother was enduring, and in anger that Al did nothing. Finally, in the wee hours of the morning, he roused himself out of bed to find a pay phone and called an ambulance. By the time my mother arrived at the hospital, her inflamed appendix had burst, spilling the infection into her abdomen and bloodstream. She was rushed to emergency surgery and treated with high doses of antibiotics. She was gravely ill and fighting for her life.

As my mother lay near death, a vague terror began to engulf me. What if she didn't come home from the hospital? What would become of me then? Each evening, Al would drink a six pack of beer, perhaps to ease his guilt. After about three nights of sleeping alone, he told me to come and sleep in the bed instead of on the floor. I protested, but he said Mommy wouldn't mind my sleeping in the comfortable bed while she was away. The night terrors immediately returned. In the darkness, the weight on me so heavy I couldn't breathe; the smell of sweat and sour breath; my small hand guided and pressed to a hot and pulsing place I knew it did not belong, until Al moaned and rolled away, soon snoring in his sleep. Now a second terror haunted me....what if Mommy finds out?!

After about ten days, I was permitted to accompany Al to the hospital to visit my mother. I was beside myself with fear, for I was sure he would tell her what a bad girl I'd been. When we arrived at the reception desk at the hospital, I promptly threw up my lunch of macaroni and cheese all over the shiny linoleum floor. Since the nurses thought I was ill, I was not allowed to see my mother, but stayed in the waiting area while Al paid her a visit. All I could think about was what she'd do to me when she found out I'd slept in her bed....and worse.

It was several weeks before my mother came home. While she was in the hospital she'd also had all her teeth removed and was fitted with a new set of dentures. When she walked through the door, I almost didn't recognize her...even thinner, with big, square, perfect white teeth...just like Bugs Bunny.

Al had fixed a special welcome home meal for her, and our lives resumed as if all was well. I lived every day waiting for the walls to come crashing down around me.

At Christmas time, I was taken to see Santa. I was now five years old and didn't believe in Santa Claus. For one thing, he was on every street corner and in every department store and was obviously a man dressed in a red suit. Besides, the only time I'd asked Santa for a present, a doll, all I got was a second hand sweater. But my mother and grandmother thought it would be fun for me to have my picture taken with Santa. I didn't like sitting on the lap of the fat man in the red suit, and made our visit short with another request for a doll.

When we picked up the photo a couple of days later, my mother and grandmother showed it to me smiling, saying how cute I looked. There I sat on Santa's knee, face turned toward the camera expressionless, with two dark purple shiners. It took a moment for the picture to register in my brain. I had two black eyes that I didn't know I had, and my mother and grandmother were pretending I didn't have them.

But when I arrived at kindergarten, the teacher took one look at me and asked my mother, "What happened to Debbie?"

"She got in a fight", my mother replied, defensively.

I stood next to her, my limp hand in hers, head hanging in shame and humiliation. I couldn't remember how or why I got two black eyes, though somewhere deep inside I knew.

My mother's unfortunate choice of babysitters only added to my humiliation. One woman tied me outside like a dog, where I was left to play unattended in the sand box. When it was time for lunch, she'd set me on the counter and shove food in my mouth, telling me to "hurry up" so she could get back to her afternoon television soap operas.

My mother next recruited a neighbor to watch me after school. She had several children for whom she had devised creative and cruel punishments, such as forcing them to squat for hours without relief, refusing them food or use of the bathroom. One day, this babysitter yelled at me for coming home from school in a big rain storm with clothes soaking wet. We were standing by the open door as she flung some trash outside.

I felt my anger rise like hot lava as I yelled back in frustration, "What was I supposed to do, fly over the puddles and between the raindrops?!" Raising my arms like wings, wishing I could fly away from this dark and dirty place.

The words were still ringing in the air as my mother rounded the corner. One look told me what I'd be in for when we crossed the gas station parking lot to our tenement apartment next door. My mother ordered me into my bedroom and to drop my pants….and my underpants. She wielded her black leather belt across my bare bottom as she had so often before, but this time I bit my lip, and refused to cry.

School had its own traumas. Arriving late meant being sent to the principal's office to have your hands smacked with a ruler. Going out on the playground often meant being teased, bullied or having your meager lunch stolen.

Use of the bathroom was viewed by our teacher as some kind of privilege, rather than a necessity. One day, my sweet neighbor Jimmy, whose gruesome mother was my babysitter, raised his hand saying, "I need to go to the basement real bad."

The teacher replied, "We're already in the basement, Jimmy", and everyone in the class roared, except me. I knew what kind of treatment he endured at home, and that this request had come only as an act of desperation. The teacher refused to let him leave our first grade classroom. A few minutes later, there was the sound of dripping, then pouring water as poor Jimmy sat in his chair peeing all over himself and the floor. His older brother was called from class to walk Jimmy home. I shuttered to think what punishment he'd receive when he arrived.

A few weeks later, as we were released from school, I realized I needed to pee before my long walk home. I told my teacher I needed to use the restroom, but she refused to let me go. I walked as quickly as I could, trying desperately to hold it. I made it to my grandparent's door, and as my hand touched the door knob, the puddle burst all over the floor.

When my grandmother opened the door, she found me standing there, crying in humiliation and fear of my mother's punishment. She did her best to calm me down, drying and rinsing me off, and finding something for me to wear. My stomach was in knots as I anticipated my mother's return from her new factory job. My grandmother never interfered in our lives, or my mother's treatment of me, but I heard her say to my mother in an imploring tone, "Betty, it wasn't her fault." My mother and I walked home in silence, my heart pounding in my chest. The incident went unpunished and was never mentioned again.

At Halloween, I was the only child in my class who didn't have a handmade or store bought costume. My mother had dressed me in her brown corduroy jacket topped by a brown paper bag with two holes cut out for eyes. My teacher pretended not to know who I was as I stood in front of her for our Halloween parade, wishing I'd stayed home from school. Prizes were given out that day. Best costume was awarded to the "retarded" girl who was twice our age and always sat quietly in a seat at the back of the room, ignored by our teacher and her classmates. That day she'd come to school wearing a fabulous clown costume her mother had made, complete with face paint, red nose and ruffled collar. I was truly happy for her recognition from the teacher and students, as her smile beamed from ear to ear. I was a little sad too, for I knew she had something far more precious. She had a mother who loved her.

But school was also a place I could shine. Reading came easily for me and I was even paraded around other classes to show off some of the words I knew and could spell. I loved to read, and helped some of my classmates who were struggling. My few "Golden Books" at home were my treasures. School was also a place I could draw and be creative, and one day the teacher gave me a treasure from her teacher closet in recognition. It was a little Christmas wreath ornament that I cherished for years.

Each time report cards came around, I received A's and B's with gold and blue good conduct stars. My grandfather gave me a shiny quarter for each A, which I gleefully added to my other birthday, chores and "Tooth Fairy" money I'd been saving. My terra cotta piggy bank with a bright flower painted on each side, was heavy with coins and nearly full. I didn't have anything in mind I wanted to buy; I simply enjoyed the comfort of its presence and was proud of how much I had saved. One day when I went to count my money, including my latest deposit, my piggy bank was empty. Not a single penny remained. I immediately ran sobbing to my mother, "My piggy bank is empty! All my money is gone!"

"Oh," she replied. "Al lost it in the poker game last night."

I felt the vile feeling of nausea and dizziness. Nothing could have replaced the meaning behind each coin, the sense of accomplishment each one represented. The subject was not raised again, and the lost poker money was never returned. I never put another dime in my piggy bank. It remained as empty as I was now feeling inside.

Then, one day, my mother mentioned that we were going to have a visitor. She was coming a long way to meet me, and I should be on my best behavior. That Saturday, there was a knock at the door and my mother invited the woman in to sit at the kitchen table. I was perched at my little table and chair in my room with the door open. They spoke in hushed tones, the visitor with a voice of authority and confidence. She seemed to be about the age of my grandmother, though much plumper, with an ample bosom. She wore a grey sweater over her navy blue blouse and full skirt that reached her ankles, a jaunty cap off to one side, and sneakers. I thought she looked quite comical, but could see she had serious business with my mother.

I don't know why, but I knew I needed to make a good impression on this lady. So I pulled out one of my favorite books, *Rumpelstiltskin*, about a girl who spun straw into gold, and began to read out loud in my best reading voice, like I did in school. I saw the woman stop speaking and turn a long gaze my way. When I finished, my mother called me to join them, introducing me to Mrs. Holloway who had come all the way from New Hampshire to meet me. They'd been discussing my going for a visit with Mrs. Holloway at her farm, and both inquired what I thought about the idea. Though I knew nothing about what my visit would entail, I quickly nodded a yes, speechless at this turn of events. And so it was settled; I would visit Holloway Farm over the Memorial weekend, just a few weeks away.

Chapter 6

June Holloway

*J*une rode home in uncustomary silence as Snow, who'd been napping in the car, chauffeured them back to Holloway Farm. There was something about the child she hadn't anticipated. She hadn't really thought anything would come of such a far-fetched idea as helping to rescue a child in jeopardy of being taken from her mother and put into foster care; not that she hadn't dealt with plenty of similar situations in her work as a psychiatric social worker. But she'd been retired from that kind of work for over a decade, dedicating her life largely to Holloway Farm.

She and Snow had taken in the lovely boy, Arthur, a former ward of the State, for a few years. Despite epilepsy, he had blossomed under their tutelage and life on the farm. But when his father came to claim him a year before he graduated high school, both Arthur and the Holloways had been sharply disappointed. Should she ever decide to take in another child, she would not repeat her prior mistake. If there ever was a next time, it would be legal and permanent.

Since her father's death the year prior, June had felt adrift. Her grief over his death and the ire she felt toward her siblings in the settling of his large estate, held equal sway in driving her moods toward darkness and despair.

Her roots were those of an old New England "blue blood" family anchored by generations of wealth, privilege and the best education money could buy, opening doors to the most prestigious positions at universities, banks and brokerage firms. Her family tree traced back to the Mayflower and a lineage that was at the pinnacle of Boston society. Family tradition dictated that the men attended Harvard University, while the women were sent to private finishing schools followed by a year abroad before returning home to marry the most appropriate match to continue the family dynasty.

June was born on January 2, 1900. Her mother had already delivered a daughter and was desperately hoping for the birth of a son, and the end of any further need to burden her tiny figure with another perilous pregnancy and delivery.

June was convinced her birth was not a welcome event, claiming the silver cup and spoon awaiting her arrival were inscribed with the name *George*. Whatever the circumstances, she, like her sister, was soon shoved into the arms of a nanny and then later a governess. When her brother was born the following January, June was pushed still further from the attentions of her busy parents; her mother running a society household, and her father working long hours and commuting by train to Boston. What attentions were directed toward the three children were lavished largely upon their handsome and delightful young son.

The children's mother, Jane, was a tiny spark of a woman, emotionally high strung and demanding. She had an "artist's temperament", was a gifted painter and had studied art in New York City and Paris. Now, as a married woman of Boston society, she oversaw a household that included cooks, maids, and coachmen. She and her husband, Lyman, had also designed and built a large summer home perched on the rocky shores of an exclusive enclave along the North Shore of Massachusetts. Jane entertained and moved among Boston's artistic and cultural circles and founded a local experimental theater bringing new and foreign plays to Boston. She was also active in the Unitarian Church, local civic and social service causes and later, the Women's Suffrage Movement. Such an engaging life left little time for mothering her three children.

As a girl and young woman, June thrived at her family's summer home where daily tennis matches, sailing around the lighthouse point, swims in the cold ocean, and plenty of intellectually stimulating companions could be found, easing the loneliness she felt back home in the suburbs of Boston. She participated in the enclave's community choir and Summer Theater, parlor games and bridge. At fifteen, her five foot five inch figure was slim and blossoming. She wore her long blond/brown hair pulled back with a ribbon, and made many of her own stylish clothes. The summer was a bustle of entertaining cousins, aunts and uncles, many of whom were well known figures in Boston. Day trips, by train and later by horseless carriage, were made to Boston for theater, ballet, symphony, and university lectures, all of which her family generously sponsored and supported.

In the fall, June, along with family and friends would rally around the Harvard versus Yale football games, wearing raccoon coats, discreetly sipping sherry to ward off the cold. By the time June was twenty two, her brother William was Harvard's quarterback. That same year, she fell in love with one of her brother's Harvard classmates. Finally, she had met someone who was her intellectual match, who traveled the same circles in society and most importantly, adored her. It was to be a brief romance.

At Christmas, June's beau asked her parent's permission for her hand in marriage; her mother absolutely forbid it. On what grounds? June never knew, other than she always felt resented by her mother. June was heartbroken and grieved for months. Finally, when she graduated from her great aunt's prestigious private school, her mother booked passage for two on a steamship to Europe. June would be spending the summer touring Europe with an aunt she loathed. June's mother would stop at nothing to nip this romance in the bud, and make June's life as miserable as possible in the process.

By Christmas the following year, June's beau was engaged to one of her cousins. Not only was her heart broken again, but she would have to share her entire summer with the neighboring lovebirds and attend their society wedding. June never forgave her mother and never found that kind of romantic and intellectual love match again.

June eventually married, at twenty four, a man who saw her as a ticket to wealth and society. Although the marriage produced a beautiful daughter, it did not last. At the time, divorce in society families was virtually unheard of. Once again, June had to face shame and humiliation and give up her dreams. She began her new life as a single mother in 1929, moving with her young daughter to an apartment in an upscale suburb of Boston, unsure how she would go on from here. The ensuing stock market crash wiped out many fortunes. But June's closest family members were able to ride out the storm and June's trust fund, though diminished, remained intact.

June pursued education as a nurse and later earned her Master's Degree in social work, becoming a charter member of the National Association of Social Workers. She took advanced studies in abnormal psychology, completing all of her doctoral studies but the presentation of her thesis dissertation.

While serving as Executive Director of a social service agency, she bought a historic farm in Sudbury, Massachusetts. It had a large antique house and barn situated on a generous parcel of farm land. The buildings and grounds had numerous hidden passageways that had been part of the northbound Underground Railroad, helping runaway slaves escape to freedom in Canada.

The owner, Snow Meader, had been forced to sell the farm as part of a nasty divorce. The farm, his herd of milking Ayrshires, his door to door milk delivery route and sales to a large local milk distributor, his very livelihood, were all gone in the sweep of one judge's dismissive hand.

Snow was at rock bottom. At age forty-seven, he'd survived being swindled out of his inheritance by his uncle. He'd found work during most of the lean, and often humiliating years of the Great Depression. He'd rebuilt his dairy business from the ground up, and now it was all gone. All he had left to his name were the few dollars in his pocket and shattered dreams.

When the buyer, June Gale invited him to stay on to help out around the place until he could get back on his feet, it was the first time he'd ever accepted a hand out, or a hand up. But he didn't see that he had any other choice. So he set up his humble living space in an empty stall in the barn, wondering what life would dish out to him next. In that moment, neither he nor June could have imagined that the future would set them on a course to share their lives together for nearly forty years.

It was during the courtship phase of their relationship that June and Snow decided to search for a new name to take into their marriage. After some genealogical research, June found an acceptable old

English name in Snow's family tree. And so when they married, they became Mr. and Mrs. Holloway. The burdens of the family names of Gale and Meader would be left behind, as they embarked on married life in the spring of 1949.

Chapter 7

The Hand of Grace

I was delivered across the doorstep of Holloway Farm under the cover of stars and the pale crescent of a new moon. The night air was heavy and perfumed with lilacs in full bloom. My uncle Wilfred carried me from the car to a small, dimly lit room. I remember being lightly tucked into a bed, among hushed whispers, and then the room going dark.

My Aunt Dorothy and her new husband had come to pick me up after work. Wilfred was related to Snow by a previous marriage, and the two were casual friends. When Snow and June acquired Holloway Farm, Willie would visit from time to time. When courting my Aunt Dorothy, he would take her on a Sunday drive to visit the Holloways, wanting to impress her with the "well to do" people he knew. It was during one of these visits that my dire situation was dropped into the conversation, and behind the scenes, my life was being shaped by seen and unseen hands.

My mother handed me over, along with a paper bag with a few clothes for my weekend visit, without a word. I was half asleep, but remember the strong smell of Wilfred's cologne as he laid me on the back seat of his mammoth black "Bat Mobile" Cadillac. With its long pointed tail fins, it was the size of a small space ship, and I was in fact being whisked away to a place unlike any I'd known my first seven years.

I awoke early the next morning with an urgent need to pee. I surveyed the room. The strangest thing about it was the hunched old refrigerator humming in the corner. On the wall was a calendar with a palomino horse and a beautiful woman smiling out over the month of May, 1961. Both were all decked out in their western finery, like a glamour shot from a movie. I got up and tentatively explored my surroundings. The adjoining room was dark and cool, trimmed with wood paneling and filled with wooden furniture and objects the likes of which I had never seen.

I needed a bathroom! There were four doors leading out of the dining room and all were closed. I began to tentatively call out, "Mrs. Holloway! Mrs. Holloway! "

Panic began to rise in my throat, that I would have an "accident".

"Mrs. Holloway! Mrs. Holloway!"

Then, I noticed in the shadows, a lovely collie dog, curled up asleep. *Lassie* was one of my favorite TV programs, and I went over to pet this dog who could have been her cousin. But when she bared her teeth at me, I quickly retreated in fear. Now the possibility of getting bitten by a strange dog, in addition to needing to pee, made my heart pound. Just then, I heard the latch and the creak of a door, and turned to see a grey haired, slightly stooped man, appearing as surprised to see me as I was to see him. I blurted out my need for a bathroom, and he led me past the dog to the bathroom. What a relief! A disaster averted!

"I'm afraid the dog will bite me!" I announced as I emerged.

"Her name is Heidi, and she is only "smiling" at you. She wouldn't hurt a fly."

The man called the dog over to us so I could pat her. She "smiled", showing her teeth again, as she slowly got up, her bushy tail wagging a gentle greeting. She was enjoying the attention. I was elated to have a new furry friend!

"Youhoo! Youhoo! Snowie! Youhoo! Youhoo! Snowie!? Would you bring me my tea?!" The voice floated down the hall.

"Oh, I must bring Mother her tea," the man said.

"Mother"? This man is as old as my grandfather and is taking care of his mother? She must be VERY old!" I thought.

"You wait here with Heidi while I fix some tea, then I'll fix you a bowl of cereal. You must be hungry."

The man stepped into the tiny galley kitchen, emerging soon with steaming cup of tea and disappeared down the hallway. I heard a short muffled exchange, and soon he returned to rummage through kitchen cupboards producing the makings of my breakfast, sending me to the refrigerator in my sleeping quarters to fetch the milk.

My cereal and juice were set out on a wooden dining table surrounded by eight solid wooden chairs that were low, hard, and uncomfortable.

"You eat your cereal while I fix Mother her breakfast."

I nodded in agreement as Heidi sat attentively beside me.

The morning before, my mother had fixed me a grilled cheese sandwich for a "special" farewell breakfast. We'd sat at the Formica table on our plastic chairs while I ate. She had gazed out the window, her thoughts elsewhere, sipping her coffee and smoking two cigarettes before I'd finished my sandwich and juice. I did not miss her at all.

In a little while, as I was struggling to finish the large glass of cold orange juice, the man reappeared and beckoned me to follow him. With some trepidation, I followed him down a narrow hallway, emerging into a bright, sun filled room. The feature attraction was a bed as big as a barge, and seated at the helm, propped up from behind with pillows, was Mrs. Holloway! She looked quite important in her quilted powder blue sleeping jacket, the blankets and quilt comfortably draped across her generous middle. The morning sun shone on her hair, framing her face in a silver halo. The large diamond ring on her hand caught the sun light, scattering beads of tiny rainbows in all directions.

She held a cup of tea aloft with an air of royalty, and motioned me to sit in the vacant chair beside the bed. I obeyed, still in awe of this most unusual spectacle. The room boasted a huge bowed window seat and a view overlooking large fields and in the distance a river. Out the window beside me I could see the lush lawn, flower gardens, more fields, a pond, and clusters of large, old trees. It was the most beautiful sight I'd ever seen.

"How did you sleep, Debbie?" Mrs. Holloway's voice brought my attention back to the room.

"Good."

"I'm glad to hear that. Snowie, bring me another cup of tea, please", and she handed off her tea cup as if to a devoted servant.

"Are you his mother?" I blurted, with unabashed curiosity.

"Oh, no, dear. That's Mr. Holloway."

"I heard him call you "Mother".

"Well, yes. That's a term of endearment. Do you know what endearment means?"

"No".

"It's a way of saying someone is special to you."

"Oh", I said, not really understanding.

Mrs. Holloway liked to talk, especially about herself and her family, and about the farm that she and Mr. Holloway had created together. I drifted in and out of attention as I longed to explore outside. Finally, after the third cup of tea, I summoned my courage.

"Can I go outside now?" I inquired hopefully.

"By all means!" And at last, I was released from our "chat".

I followed Mr. Holloway to the door, stepping out into the most glorious day of my young life. Heidi trotted off down the hill toward the huge barn, as I followed on her heels. A sweet pungent odor greeted me as I peered in over the Dutch door and two barn cats skittered by as I opened it. Shafts of light created a checkerboard pattern on the sawdust strewn floor and spotlighted dusty, draping cobwebs.

The barn was empty of cows. One lonely bull stood in his stanchion. He was a huge beast, black and white, though the white was really brown with caked on manure. He turned his head my way, a large metal ring in his nose. I felt bad for him all alone in the dark barn, and was certain that ring in his nose must really hurt. I walked slowly toward him and reached out to pat his enormous head with its white crown of horns.

"Betta be caffle theyah!" A voice warned, and I nearly jumped out of my skin.

"That's Elocke. He don't mean yah no harm, but one swipe of his head could knock yah down or worse. I'm Jeb Trombley. You can call me Jeb. Who are you?"

I looked down sheepishly. "I'm Debbie. I'm visiting Mr. and Mrs. Holloway. I didn't mean to do nothin' wrong."

"So you like animals, hey?"

"Yah, I guess so."

"Well, how about we go visit the calves…they're more your size."

"Okay!"

I followed mutely past Elocke, out a side door into a small corral. There were several calves – some brown and white, some black and white, and one that looked like a deer with its fawn colored coat, huge dark eyes and black wet nose.

"Are these your calves?"

"Well, yes they are. The Holloways sold their cows a year ago and had this big empty barn. So I rent the barn from them and live in the apartment upstairs with my wife. Would you like to feed the calves some grain?"

"Sure!"

Jeb returned with a bucket and I was nearly toppled over as the calves rushed over to poke their heads in for a snack. When the bucket was empty, I visited each one stroking their silky necks. The paddock was muddy from recent rain and fresh cow manure, but I loved the smell of the animals, their touch and how I felt around them.

Just then I heard Mrs. Holloway calling … "Debbie! Debbie! Come in please. We've got some errands to do."

"Would you like to watch the cows get milked later?"

"Sure!"

"Well, if it's okay with Mrs. Holloway, come on back around 4:00. That's when I call the girls in for milkin' and feedin' time."

"Okay, I will"! I hurried back up to the house.

Mr. and Mrs. Holloway were gathering themselves for a trip into town and led me out to the car. They referred to their car as *The Imperial*. It was teal and chrome with a creamy leather interior. I had never ridden on a cloud before! I gazed out the window as we drove up the bumpy gravel road through fields dotted with horses and cows, emerging on a winding paved road. Pitched roofed Cape Cod houses and grand square colonials peered out along the street with half shut eyes, many having surveyed passersby for more than two hundred years. Old spreading maples and a few stately elms had held their posts even longer.

We arrived at the local hardware store where Mr. Holloway purchased an assortment of nails and screws for various projects, some dog food and a new paintbrush. He seemed to delight over his small purchases like a child in a candy store.

Then it was on to the grocery store where we cruised up and down each aisle. Now and again Mrs. Holloway would ask me, "Would you like some of this? Do you like these? "

When we got to the canned food aisle she asked me to pick out something for lunch. I surveyed the shelves and finally selected what looked like a familiar item. By the time we had made our rounds, the shopping cart was heaped with food....bread, eggs, milk, cheeses, fresh fruits and vegetables, cereals, orange marmalade, all kinds of prepared and frozen foods, TV dinners (a dozen of those), packages of cookies, quarts of ice cream, nuts, candy. The bill came to over fifty dollars! I had never seen so much food at one time. It turned out Mrs. Holloway was a big fan of canned and frozen foods, as she loathed cooking.

Back at Holloway Farm, Mrs. Holloway heated the canned beans and franks. A single place was set for me and the steaming bowl was served. I don't know why I chose those beans and franks. They tasted terrible! The little hot dogs were squirmy and had a foul odor. I had gone hungry plenty of times and was not a picky eater, but this stuff was gross! I picked at my meal hoping Mrs. Holloway would take pity on me and offer me something else – like a peanut butter and jelly sandwich.

But instead she said, "Well, I see you're a slow eater. So you stay here until you finish your lunch. Then you can go outside to play.

My heart sank into my empty stomach. I picked at the meal, bean by bean until all that was left were the disgusting and squirmy little hot dogs. Heidi, seeming to know of my plight came and sat attentively at my side. In a flash I knew salvation had arrived! Very discreetly, I spooned one of the slippery little hot dogs into my napkin and then let it slip onto the floor, where Heidi eagerly woofed it down. As I was about to drop the third torpedo, Mrs. Holloway reappeared to check on my progress.

"Oh", she crooned, as my heart pounded in my ears, "I see you're almost finished. We always eat what is on our plate. It's not polite to leave food you have been served." And she disappeared again.

My heart continued to skip a beat. I don't know what would have happened if she had caught me giving my food to the dog. I know what would happen back home in Worcester. It would be grounds for a good spanking and no supper.

Finally, the last slimy torpedo disappeared, thanks to Heidi's eager assistance. I brought my empty bowl into the kitchen and went out to explore more of Holloway Farm. Across the dirt road from the farm were acres of field in bloom with clover, alfalfa and wild flowers. Butterflies glimmered here and there. I'd never seen butterflies before and I immediately was in another world. I lost track of time following them from flower to flower and trying to catch one.

Finally, the spell was broken as I heard Jeb call to me, "Debbie! It's milkin' time!"

I hurried back to the barn and stood out of the way as he called in "the girls". Like a carefully choreographed line dance, the cows merged into an orderly bovine procession, with lots of excited "mooing". Stragglers came trotting or galloping; their pendulous, swollen udders swaying awkwardly like giant water balloons ready to burst. I watched in amazement as each cow went into her appointed station where her ration of feed awaited.

Jeb went down the line closing each stanchion. He did not keep the cleanest of barns, and I felt sad for the cows being so confined and standing on cold, bare cement. Many cows were caked with mud and manure. But to me, they had a sweet smell as I walked down the center aisle trying to pat and touch their massive heads. One cow caught my attention; she was "pink" (a red roan I later learned). She was like the grandmother of the herd, calm and gentle. She allowed me to pat her and tell her how pretty she was. I called her Lizzie Tish.

Jeb had disappeared into the milking parlor and came out with a milking machine. The contraption looked like a torture device as he strapped it around the cow's middle. Bringing his milking stool alongside, he washed her udder in iodine disinfectant, attached the machine to her teats and the suction of the machine began to pump her milk into the stainless steel container. The electric machine pumped in a rhythmic pulse, sounding like it was gasping for air. The milking machine was a cold stand in for the nursing calves, now being fed milk replacement and grain. The milk from these cows would soon be on the shelves of grocery stores throughout New England.

As Jeb sat hunched at his stool, the cow flicked her manure caked tail across his face. He seemed oblivious, lost in his milking meditation. Down the line on both sides of the barn the ritual was repeated. Now and again, a cow would grimace at the tenderness of her gorged udder and kick out sideways. One big black and white Holstein hit her mark and knocked Jeb off his stool onto the wet, smelly cement. He gave her a swift smack on her rump and yelled "Get up theyah! God damn yah! " The cow froze, the whites of her eyes shining like crescent moons as a slight tremor rippled along her flank. Finally, she resumed eating, relaxed and "dropped her milk".

Two cats shadowed Jeb, and finally as he was finishing off the milking of a cow by hand, he aimed her teat at the big grey tiger. The first two shots hit him in the face. Then he opened his mouth as Jeb aimed the stream of milk from the teat again. I laughed out loud at this antic! Both cats had learned how to have a special treat at milking! Later, Jeb would put out a bowl of milk. That was their only food, as these were barn cats, expected to keep down the rodent population. Hungry cats were better hunters. There was a peacefulness and calm as the cows all chomped on their forage to the steady rhythm of the milking machine. The fragrances of sweet silage, hay, manure and iodine blended into an earthy aroma that was somehow comforting. I thought I would burst with new found joy!

The Memorial Day weekend was over all too soon. By mid-day Monday, I was riding in the back seat on the creamy leather seats, with June and Snow Holloway at the helm, driving me back to Worcester, my heart shrinking with every mile.

When we arrived, my mother came out to meet us, a blank expression on her face. I couldn't tell what any of this had been about, and I felt my eyes stinging with tears at the thought of never visiting Holloway Farm again. Mr. Holloway stood by silent, looking down at the ground. Mrs. Holloway was chatty and all aglow about how well the visit had gone, and how nicely I had settled in. Finally, there was a lull and no one spoke. I was standing next to my mother, digging the toe of my shoe in the dirt when her words fell like prayers from heaven.

"Do you want to go live with the Holloways?"

"Yes!" I replied, without a moment's hesitation.

"Yes, please, yes", my heart silently echoed, as it pounded, nearly bursting with joy at this turn of events.

Chapter 8

A New Life

*O*n a Saturday in June, after the close of my first year of school, I sat on the worn stoop of our Worcester tenement, eagerly awaiting my return to Holloway Farm. Mr. and Mrs. Holloway arrived late morning. After a brief visit with my mother, they packed my few belongings into the car. I was so eager to go, I nearly forgot to say goodbye to my mother. Mrs. Holloway assured her she was welcome to visit any time.

As the miles rolled by, I felt lighter and lighter. My heart fluttered in anticipation and my stomach churned, for once not with hunger, but with excitement. Heidi greeted us in the driveway, and I ran to the barn to greet the cows, and tell Lizzie Tish that I had come to live at Holloway Farm!

That summer was a dream. I felt like I had stepped into a fairy tale. I didn't know how or why my life had taken such a turn, but I knew it was a true miracle. And I intended to make the most of it.

The first morning of my return, Snowie said, "Mornin, Deb. I think you might want to go have a look in the stables." I raced out to the carriage shed, and to my amazement and delight, there were two beautiful ponies munching hay in their stalls! Without hesitation and with no prior experience whatsoever, I clipped a lead rope on one of the pony's halters and led her outside to hand graze on the clover. Snow watched, saying nothing, a light smile creeping across his face. I was in heaven; there was no doubt about it!

Snow told me how he and June had gone to a local auction and purchased the two ponies for fifty dollars. They had been shipped in from the west, were extremely thin and had just recovered from shipping fever. But they were young and sound; Snow had been able to fatten them up in no time. Bay Lady, "Lady", was a dark mahogany bay, with a long black mane and forelock to the tip of her muzzle, her thick tail nearly touched the ground. The only white were two jagged horizontal stripes across both front legs, where she no doubt had gotten tangled in barbed wire. The cuts must have been deep for the hair to grow in white. She had very refined features, a beautifully chiseled head, and fine delicate legs, looking more like a miniature horse than a pony. Her stable mate, "Cindy", for "cinders", due to her jet black color, was built like a small tank, with not one speck of white.

That summer I immediately set about learning to ride, though neither the ponies nor I knew a thing about it. My lessons began with the basics of how to care for the ponies and work around them safely.

Every day, I would bring them out to the cross ties to carefully groom them, learning how to pick out their hooves, feed them and muck out their stalls. To start, we had a well-worn western saddle and bridle left over from the previous farm pony, Spud, who had recently died at age 30, having helped start many a young rider.

My first attempts at riding were dismal. Each pony had a very effective strategy for removing me from their back. Lady had a lot of spirit and simply waited until I was aboard, counted to ten, and commenced to buck. Without much effort on her part, I was soon sitting in the dust while she trotted to the nearest patch of grass for a snack. Snowie even bravely got on hoping to dull her efforts with his adult size and weight. She bucked him off before they were half way around the little fenced sheep paddock we were using as our riding ring.

Cindy's approach was to embark at a brisk trot until I bounced off or, if that didn't work, simply to rub me off along the fence. What neither the ponies nor I knew at the start was that I possessed a fierce determination to ride! I was not going to be deterred by their bad behavior. One day after being thrown and landing hard three times, I rose with angry tears streaming down my face, yelling to my wayward pony, "I'm going to ride you!"

Though I was ready to climb back on, Mrs. Holloway intervened saying, "That's enough for one day. You can try again tomorrow."

Each evening while I ate my supper on the screened porch, Mrs. Holloway would read to me from *Learning to Ride*. It was a beautiful book with photographs of a girl about my age and her grey Welsh pony, leading me step by step thru the care of my pony, to riding and even showing. This gave me further incentive to do my very best. Soon, a properly fitting English saddle and bridles were purchased. I rode on a lead line and then a long lunge line until the ponies learned to accept me as rider, responding to my voice, legs and reins. Before long, I was comfortably in charge of both ponies at a walk and a trot, and soon was riding the country road and trails with more experienced neighbor children. If anyone else got on to ride either pony, they immediately resorted to their old tactics.

When I wasn't riding, I was visiting the cows, and spending endless hours exploring the fields and pastures trying to capture a butterfly or two in an old peanut butter jar. There were also weekly swimming lessons at the local recreation center in town. I'd been given art supplies and happily spent many hours drawing and coloring. I'd even painted rocks for the garden, though being watercolors, my efforts were washed away with the first rain.

The neighbor children were several years older than me, but that didn't stop us from spending endless hours together. They took me under their wing, and we went blueberry picking and rode the trails along the edge of the hay fields. On rainy days they taught me card games, or we would color in my *National Velvet* coloring books or browse some of the many horse books. At night I'd fall asleep to the haunting call of the whippoorwills and the rising chorus of crickets, counting my blessings which were now as numerous as the stars.

In late August, it was agreed I could enter the local 4-H horse show. I registered for several classes and came home with a second place red ribbon in the Beginner Equitation class where the rider is being judged on her form, posture, and how well she guides her mount through its paces. All my hard knocks and efforts had paid off! I was very proud of my accomplishment, and of Cindy who had proven to be reliable and unflappable in this new experience of riding in a ring with other horses and ponies. I displayed my ribbon in my room with a picture taken on that day, and dreamed of becoming an even better rider and coming home with the blue ribbon and trophy next time.

Mrs. Holloway had other ambitions for me besides learning to ride. Every morning while she had her breakfast in bed followed by several cups of tea, I was given lessons in speaking correct English with proper diction. To expand my vocabulary she would pull words from the Reader's Digest magazine and teach me their meaning and spelling. She would sometimes read aloud, and often spend hours telling me about her life and her prestigious family.

When Snowy was present, the stories were more interesting to me, involving animals, farming and his boyhood in Maine. But ours was an awkward relationship, as he'd not been raised to believe children should be doted on; rather, they should be seen and not heard and be put to good use with plenty of chores to earn their keep. In his eyes, I was being spoiled and not pulling my weight. Having a young child in the household was the last thing Snow wanted or expected, especially so soon after the death of Mr. Gale, whom he'd adored as the father he'd never had. June had not even consulted Snow on the matter of my arrival, and this only added to his resentment of my presence. Mrs. Holloway instructed me that I was now to call her Aunt June, and Mr. Holloway I was to call Snow or Snowie, as everyone did, including children.

Aunt June had sewn several versions of what would be my summer uniform that year - shorts, and coordinating sleeveless tops fashioned out of colorful fabrics, my favorite featuring puppies peeking out of a hat box. Footwear was generally coordinating sneakers, except for when riding, when sturdy shoes with heels were required, along with jeans and a hard hat. She cut my hair herself, into a short Dutch boy style, with short, crookedly cut bangs that I hated. I was chubby and the cut of my hair and clothing did nothing to hide that fact. I tried not to let it bother me, but I knew I would be a target for teasing when it came time for school.

As summer was waning, Aunt June announced I could have a party to celebrate my eighth birthday. In fact, there would be two parties! One for children my age, and one for the older neighbor friends I played and rode the trails with. We bought the invitations and I wrote, addressed, and stamped each one, placing them expectantly in the mailbox for the postman. I grew more and more excited as the replies accepting my invitation began to arrive in the mail.

When my birthday arrived on September 1st, I could hardly wait for the appointed time! I helped to set out the snacks and activities, arrange the chairs, and decorate and set the table. Finally, everything was ready and I sat watching the clock count down the time until the party would begin. Finally, my new found friends began to arrive, and we got right into the party games with prizes to entertain us. It was a beautiful day so we all went outside to play ball and try our hand at badminton and croquet.

Later, Aunt June announced dessert would be served and we rushed inside where we were served bowls of ice cream and cookies. I heard some of the children whisper, "Where's the birthday cake? Isn't she going to have a birthday cake and candles on her birthday?"

After the ice cream, I opened my presents, a pink fluffy kitty in a basket, coloring books, a pink sweater and my favorites – a beautiful bone china mare and her foal. One party ended and the second began with my older friends. We played outside until near dark. As they sat on the ground, I hid behind the giant thorn tree and pretending I was on the radio, sang my version of *Summer Time,* which I'd heard recently at a Summer Theater production of *Porgy and Bess.* Everyone applauded in stunned surprise.

That night as Aunt June tucked me into bed, I inquired, "Why didn't we have a birthday cake and candles for my party?"

"I don't believe in such nonsense as cake and candles for your birthday", she briskly replied, turning out the light.

71

I didn't believe in Santa Clause or the Easter Bunny, but I did believe in birthday cakes, even though I'd never had one. Although the parties had been lots of fun, and I had received wonderful gifts, I couldn't make the sharp pang of disappointment go away. There would be one more birthday party when I turned thirteen, a very creative treasure hunt; but there would be no cake or candles, and this time, none had been expected. I would be a grown woman before I had my first birthday cake with candles …. and birthday wishes too!

When school started in September, my friends and I walked the country lane to catch the bus. I had a brand new pencil box with sharpened pencils, erasers, and a Black Beauty lunch box. I was eager to start second grade. I soon learned all the other children had attended first grade together and that as an outsider, I would have to earn any degree of acceptance. The teacher was critical and dismissive of me, and my eager anticipation of returning to school soon turned to dread. When I came home in tears with a paper marked up with a red pen and my first "C", Mrs. Holloway made an appointment to see my teacher. Whatever transpired, I didn't feel as picked on by the teacher after that. While I made no real friends at school that year, I thrived in the friendships I had with my neighbors who didn't object to my being from "away", or being several years younger either.

As Christmas approached, I was beside myself with anticipation. I crafted special cards for Aunt June and Snow and a book of drawings – animals, trees, the ponies. I could hardly wait to surprise them with my creations. We hung fresh sprigs of greens around the house and hung wreathes with a red bow on all the doors, including those in the carriage shed and dairy barn. We put a single white candle light in each window of the house and when the first snow arrived, it turned Holloway Farm into a Currier & Ives postcard. But one important thing was missing, and I began to wonder if Aunt June didn't believe in Christmas trees and presents either.

The week before Christmas, we began preparing for the Christmas Eve service at the local Unitarian church by shopping for toys which would later be distributed to poor children in the community. Mrs. Holloway let me pick out several toys for girls and boys, and we came home with two large bags. We wrapped them all in white tissue paper with red ribbon, and labeled them for a girl or boy and the age. Aunt June had sewn me a new red velvet dress for the holidays. She donned her best hand sewn wool coat with matching hat and gloves, and Snow wore his one "best" suit for the occasion.

The church and its tall spire shone white in the crisp winter moon light. Inside, it glowed by candle light, with real candles surrounded by greens in each of the tall, deeply set windows and in grouped arrangements. Beside the pulpit were two of the tallest Christmas trees I'd ever seen, glowing with white lights and sparkling ornaments. Snow found us a seat while Aunt June and I placed the presents under the trees, adding to the large piles already growing there. I felt such a warm glow all over from the beauty of the church, and the generosity of spirit.

I didn't care if there was no tree or presents at home. The way I felt inside, I knew this was what the true Christmas spirit was all about.

The minister gave a short sermon, followed by carols and our forming a circle around the sanctuary, each lighting our own candle, and singing Silent Night. I could not remember a time of such incredible joy and beauty. Following the service, everyone was invited to the parsonage for hot chocolate, cookies and more caroling. Our hearts were warm and our cheeks rosy by the time we walked the short distance into the welcoming warmth and good cheer.

I was quiet all the way home. Words couldn't describe the many feelings of joy and awe I felt that night. Shortly after we arrived back at Holloway Farm, Snowie handed me one of his large lumberman's wool stockings to hang on the fireplace. I took this as a promising sign! Soon, I was fast asleep not knowing what Christmas Day might bring.

The next morning when I came downstairs, to my astonishment, the door beside the fireplace was open to a room I didn't know existed. At the center was a tall Christmas tree, covered top to bottom with glass ornaments of every description, as well as animals and birds, garlands and multi colored lights. And beneath the tree were a dazzling number of wrapped presents! June and Snow had set up a little sitting area for opening the gifts. Since it was still early and Snow and Aunt June wouldn't be up for a couple hours, I decided to take a closer look. And yes! Many of the packages were for me! And there, hanging from the fireplace, was the stocking, stuffed with surprises! I ran upstairs to get my hand made cards and book of drawings and placed them under the tree, wishing I had more to offer.

Finally, the time came to open my stocking and gifts, and I took my time with each one, still not believing it was true. The stocking was a treasure trove of magical little toys and stuffed animals, wee games, a harmonica, a miniature paint set, candy and a customary tangerine in the toe. Among the presents was a watercolor paint set with 100 different colors and paper and brushes too; several books including *The Lonesome Little Colt* about an orphan foal; school clothes, a winter coat, a small sled and new brushes and halters for Lady and Cindy. Snow and June exchanged a few gifts and seemed delighted with my hand made offering.

In the afternoon we had Christmas dinner with our next door neighbors who were now renting Pasture House. We children accompanied by Heidi spent much of the afternoon playing outside in the snow. That evening, I helped Snowie prepare a hot bran mash with apples and carrots, as a special holiday meal for Lady and Cindy. Heidi, still wearing her red Christmas bow, lay snoring by the fire as Aunt June read aloud to me, *The Lonesome Little Colt.* He's a lucky little colt because he finds a new mother to care for him and keep him safe. And as I drifted off to sleep that night, I knew I was one very, very lucky little girl too.

That was the best Christmas…Ever!

Chapter 9

The End of a Beautiful Dream

*A*s the months rolled by, I did wonder from time to time why I had not heard from any of my Worcester relatives. No phone calls, letters or gifts arrived from my mother, grandparents or my Aunt Dorothy. What I didn't know at the time, was that Aunt June had discreetly discarded all cards, letters and packages addressed to me. She'd also been slowly removing any belongings reminding her of my origins – my large pink stuffed poodle from my Aunt Dorothy was confiscated and donated to more "needy" children, along with my favorite sweater, which had been "accidently" thrown in the dryer where it shrank to several sizes too small.

I don't remember feeling sad or lonely, though I wished I didn't have to sleep upstairs in an attic bedroom at the opposite end of the house from where the Holloways slept. Although there were no wasp nests or mice, when darkness fell, the room was pitch black, and I was sure if I cried out from a bad dream or was revisited by nightmares, no one would hear me.

That spring there was a surprise visit. My mother and Al drove up from Worcester on the Easter weekend, in his old jalopy. They arrived during the spring flood and when Al tried to ford the swollen river waters, the car stalled out mid-stream. He, wearing a thrift store suit two sizes too small, and my mother in a new peach colored dress, carrying her matching shoes and handbag high, waded thru the muck and knee deep water. They came to the door a sorry sight, and I felt really bad for them, especially my mother. I could tell she wanted to make a good impression on Mrs. Holloway for whatever reasons. I also knew she didn't have a prayer in Hell of doing so.

I could see there was a game of cat and mouse going on, and I was the prize. June Holloway had set her sights on having me in her life permanently, but first she would string my mother along with talk of how much she must have missed me, and how hard it must be to raise a child alone, and how committed she was to my having a good education and opportunities. She only wanted what was best for me, for all of us, implying that if I went back to live with my mother, she would finance my future. But nothing could have been further from the truth.

All I knew was I did not miss my mother or Al one bit, and that I definitely did not want to go back to Worcester ever again. The visit was short, over a cup of tea and biscuits. Snow then set about towing the car to dry land with the tractor, and he and Al finally got it started for the long, cold drive back to Worcester. I went to bed that night with a hollow feeling in the pit of my stomach, not knowing what the future would bring. I knew my mother was also thinking about what a future with some of Mrs. Holloway's money would look like. I was pretty sure it was a future that wouldn't have much to do with me.

That summer we had other guests who ended up staying until fall, while their newly purchased old farmhouse was renovated and made livable. These were cousins of Aunt June's and best of all, they had two children including a girl, Jane, just a year older than me. What a blessing to have a live-in play mate! Jane was like a shooting star, full of life, laughter and a sense of adventure that far surpassed my own. She was the light of my summer, leading me on excursions and adventures around the farm.

We took the ponies down to the river for swims, ate blueberries until our tummies burst, and made blueberry pancakes and muffins with the ones we managed to bring home. Jane was a fabulous artist even at a young age, and we shared our passion for drawing and painting. We'd lie out on the lawn at night gazing up at the stars, imagining what our lives would be like when we were older. I cried myself to sleep the night Jane and her family packed up their belongings to move into their own home. Even though she would be living only a few miles away, it would not be the same….the same as almost having a sister.

We did see quite a lot of our cousins that summer, and one weekend I was packed up to join Jane for a visit to her grandparents who owned a home right on the beach. What a glorious time! Sunshine, digging, and collecting shells and beach stones of every color imaginable; catching small crabs and releasing them back in the tide pools; the cool breeze blowing in our hair; and the taste of salt air on sunburned skin. We ate supper of fresh fish accompanied by her grandmother's fabulous "from scratch home cooking" on the screened porch, with the sound of the waves churning across the pebble beach, as gulls glided by sideways on the sea wind.

That evening we looked thru Jane's 3D View Master at amazing images from places around the world and poured over books on travel and art from her grandmother's collection.

We shared a bedroom, telling stories and laughing until we finally fell asleep in happy exhaustion. That weekend was one of the sweetest in memory, and Jane was my inspiration and best-friend-sister-cousin. Later that summer, we ceremonially cut our hands, pressing our bloody palms together, and became true "blood cousins".

What I didn't know, was that my life was about to take another radical turn, and all the cherished friendships I had made were about to be torn asunder. Holloway Farm, the place that I adored and called home, the place that was a healing balm to my mind, body and soul; the place that had given me so many happy and joyful memories in such a short time; the place I wanted to live the rest of my life....Holloway Farm.....had been sold! In fact, the farm had been for sale the entire time I'd lived there, and never a word spoken. June broke the news to me one morning over a cup of tea, during our daily "chat". She gave no reason, instructing me in a matter of fact tone I should start packing up my belongings; we were moving to a farm near a big lake, about two hours away.

Her words fell like shards of glass around me. I felt the earth open up and swallow some part of me I couldn't name. My dreams shattered and some place in my heart snapped shut rather than feel the pain of it all. It was simply too much to bear. Each night I cried myself to sleep, in my heart asking, "Why, why, why, was I given so much, only to have what I dearly loved taken away?

This is a question I would ask myself again and again over the years. Decades later, while engaged in shamanic studies and self-healing, I would learn how the energy of trauma can pass generation to generation...and from life time to life time. I would uncover the soul wounds that had been recreating this pattern of loss and suffering in my life, again and again. And, more importantly, I would learn how to clear and heal these wounds, for myself and others.

But until then, this pattern of being uprooted would be repeated with regularity and intensity, especially around "home" and any and all "relationships". I was locked in the grip of generational and past life wounds held deep within my subconscious "mind" and soul memory. I did not yet realize these were the core wounds I had come into this lifetime to heal, or that I would find the keys for unlocking the gates to my suffering, and for setting myself free.

It would take several months for the sale of Holloway Farm to go through, so I started third grade in Amherst, walking to the bus with my friends. But now, I was heavy with the sadness and dread of what was coming.

Mrs. Holloway was leasing out the large ell and huge barn of the Mirror Lake property to a couple who raised champion Arabian horses; and she'd already had the main house renovated to suit her needs.

On weekends, we began to move smaller items to Mirror Lake. After school on Friday, we'd make the long drive, arriving in the dark. I would help Snow offload the truck, struggling to untie the frozen knots in the ropes securing the load, and to carry the heavy items into the barn. Meanwhile, June would turn up the furnace, start a fire in the sitting room fireplace and heat up some TV dinners for supper. I could tell Snow was devastated by having to move, and clearly had not been consulted in the decision. I felt numb from the cold...and the ache in my heart at leaving the farm and my friends in Amherst.

In November, the movers arrived, removing all that was left of our lives in Amherst. The house, carriage shed, dairy barn and out buildings stood empty. Snow had delivered the ponies to Mirror Lake during the week, and at least they would be waiting for us upon our arrival. Dear old Heidi had been put down just a few weeks earlier, and I was still grieving her loss, and the fact that Aunt June insisted we just drop her off at the vet. I couldn't get the hollow feeling out of my heart, how my sweet friend had been abandoned by all of us in her final hours.

Our last day at Holloway Farm, Amherst, was Thanksgiving Day. We stood in the empty house, using the bathroom counter off the magnificent master bedroom as a perch for some packaged peanut butter crackers and juice as our farewell and holiday meal. I could hardly get a crumb of food down as I fought back the tears.

I would never set foot on Holloway Farm again, except in my imagination. I wanted to hold it forever in my heart as it was during this fleeting time in my childhood.

In just a few short years, the entire river valley was to become road kill, run over by subdivisions with names like River View and Blueberry Lane. One farm remained intact as a golf course, but most sold out to developers. In less than seven years, there wasn't one dairy farm left standing in the valley. Then one day, the massive dairy barn that had once housed my sweet Lizzie Tish and her bovine companions, and a herd of prized Jerseys, burned to the ground. All the fire trucks from several surrounding towns were called to put out the flames leaping one hundred feet high. The barn was empty, and rumors spread that the fire had been deliberately set. But the heart sometimes refuses to let go. So I only remember Holloway Farm as it was when I knew it; when I stepped from a nightmare into a short lived, but beautiful dream.

We are born with a natural sense of wonder and curiosity. We learn through all our senses, exploring our world through touch, sights, sounds and smells, following our intuitive desire to "know the world" on our own terms. We learn through trial and error, first by emulating those around us, and then by exploring new directions on our own.

Often those around us seek to guide us in directions not in alignment with who we truly are. We may find ourselves following or even forced onto a path not of our choosing. Yet, none of us can really fit comfortably in someone else's shoes for very long. We are not meant to live the life someone else dreams for us. We are meant to live the life we have dreamed for ourselves. — *Debra LightHeart*

Chapter 10

Adopted!

We settled into our lives in Mirror Lake and I entered my new school mid-term. I quickly made friends with two neighbors, and enrolled in the local 4-H Club. In addition to the two ponies that I was beginning to outgrow, the Holloways purchased a yearling colt from a friend who raised Arabians. I can still remember the first time I saw him napping in his stall. He was a lovely creature and reminded me of a deer. He stood, shaking himself off, and came over to greet us. He was copper chestnut, with a large star and a small white snip on the tip of his muzzle. Each hind sock had a brown spot right in the center and a corresponding black stripe down the white hooves; his mane and tail were flaxen. His name was Radsun, and it was love at first sight. I devoted countless hours grooming his copper coat, and basic training to gain his trust and teach him good manners. My time with Radsun and the ponies focused my attention and temporarily set me free from any worries about my future.

One day, Mrs. Holloway sat me down for some "games". I didn't know at the time they were series of tests she had used during her days as a social worker. They tested IQ, aptitudes, social skills, creativity and emotional and psychological stability or lack thereof.

Soon after, I was taken to a pediatrician for a very complete physical. Near the end of my check-up, I was put on the examining table completely naked. The doctor was chatting away, telling amusing stories. Then with his finger, he took a quick poke between my legs. My "physical" was over and I was allowed to get dressed.

I was being thoroughly vetted. June wanted to be sure I would be worth her investment, and that I had not been too badly "damaged" during the abusive first six years of my life. As a professionally trained and experienced social worker, she knew only too well the lasting emotional scars that often form as a result of early trauma.

It was a relief when the doctor assured her I was still a virgin. The other tests showed that I was well above average in intelligence and creativity, and this pleased her equally well. Looking back, I have no doubt if I had "failed" any of the tests, I would have been sent packing back to Worcester "as quick as the shake of a lamb's tail."

As it turned out, my mother took the upper hand on that account. One evening there was a phone call, and when Mrs. Holloway hung up the phone, my heart sank to me feet. My mother wanted me back.

When school closed for the Christmas holidays, I was driven by Snow and some friends back to Worcester. June stayed home unable to make the heart-wrenching trip. She was very careful to pack me up with pretty much the same belongings I'd arrived with. I wasn't allowed to bring any of my new books, clothes, toys or art supplies. The one exception was my guinea pig, Miss Whitey Brown. I was allowed to bring her along in her little cage.

I went out to the barn to say goodbye to the Lady, Cindy and Radsun, tears streaming down my face. I'd already told my friends I wouldn't be at school when they came back from the holidays. I sat in the back seat with Miss Whitey Brown on my lap, and didn't say a word during the long drive back to Worcester.

My mother tried to be a better mother, and didn't hit me anymore. She asked me what was "different" about living with the Holloways. How could I tell her everything was different?! I finished out third grade in Worcester, with a teacher I feared and loathed. Everything we did was "timed", and for the first time, I was no longer coming home with A's and B's on my report card. I'd attended three schools during my third grade year, and was relieved when the Worcester session finally let out for the summer. But I was anxious with fear and worry as my life and future continued to hang in limbo.

As the months rolled by, there was no word from the Holloways. Even worse, as far as my mother was concerned, there were no offers of money to help take care of me. When a call came in from her latest boyfriend, saying he'd be released from prison in a few weeks, after doing time for writing bad checks, I knew my fate was sealed. I would be chattel around my mother's neck once her boyfriend was back in the picture. I had met this man a few times before. He was a handsome, blue eyed, charming con man who liked to poke and tease me for amusement. Once again, I felt the walls of terror closing in on me.

But my mother opted for a fresh start, this time without a child to thwart her chances at romance. She called Mrs. Holloway, and it was arranged that I should go back to Holloway Farm. But this time, Mrs. Holloway insisted, she wanted to legally adopt me. She promised my mother that she and my family could still see me whenever they wanted. My life once again shifted toward new possibilities. When school let out for the summer, I was sent once more to live with the Holloways, and this time it would be for good!

June set about doing all the paperwork, and getting the referrals and documentation she would need to persuade a judge to agree to this rather unusual circumstance. First of all, she and Snow were in their mid-sixties; I had lived with my natural mother for the better part of eight years; and another relative (my aunt) had offered to adopt me already, but my mother had refused. By now, there was also an active file with my name on it with Child Welfare and Protective Services. If I wasn't sent to live with the Holloways, there was a good chance I'd be placed into foster care. So June did her homework, got an adoption lawyer, found respectable people to give reasons and references as to why I should be allowed to be adopted by the Holloways.

One day Aunt June sat me down and told me in a rather formal tone what her promises and expectations would be upon my adoption. She would never hit me and she would pay for me to have a good education. She instructed me I was now to call her "Mother", and to continue to call Snow, "Snow" or "Snowie". I was deeply disappointed at this bit of news, as I'd had my heart set on finally having my very own "Daddy".

June further instructed me, "I was not to grow up too fast"so she, Snowie and I would have more years together, since we'd missed sharing my first seven years. I was too young to have a clue how this genuinely flawed and unrealistic expectation would impact and eventually devastate our lives in just a few short years.

Finally, the big day came, and we drove to the courthouse. I was made to wait in the car for what seemed like hours. Finally, I had to pee….I had to pee bad… I watched the clock. Surely, they would be coming back any minute. The car was in the large parking lot outside the looming courthouse building. I had no idea where to go, and was afraid of what would happen if I wasn't in the car when they returned on this, my adoption day. I was too embarrassed to get out of the car and pee outside. Finally, I couldn't hold on any longer. June's new Chrysler 300 had a metal console in the back. I straddled it hoping it would contain some of my pee, tears streaming down my face in fear and shame, as my new outfit was soaked.

A few minutes later June and Snow returned to the car, to discover my accident.

They retrieved some towels from the trunk of the car and matter-of-factly wiped up as best they could. Then we found a general store and purchased a very unflattering change of clothes for me to wear for the remainder of my adoption day.

We were on our way to some friends of the family to celebrate my adoption, but my excitement and anticipation for the big day had already been dashed, and would soon be shattered. When we arrived, June promptly told everyone gathered how I'd wet myself in the car, and that I had done it deliberately, in anger at being made to wait in the car so long! I couldn't believe my ears, as the blood rushed to my face, and anger coursed through my veins. I looked at the floor wishing it would open and simply swallow me up.

After that day, whenever we arrived anywhere, I had an immediate urge to pee. We'd arrive at a friend's house, at a party, or go out for a meal, or stop to pick something up at the store, and I urgently needed the bathroom. My humiliation over that one event haunted me for many months to come.

I was ever so glad to pick up life on the farm once more. Every day, I was in the barn grooming the ponies and the beautiful new colt. He had grown while I was away and was gentle but full of fire as

Arabians naturally are. I loved to watch him gallop across the field, his tail flagging over his back, as he seemed to float across the ground on air, tossing his head and snorting like a wild horse. Then the best thrill of all, when he'd come prancing up to me and dip his black velvet muzzle to sniff my hair and outstretched hand.

Since I'd shown such serious interest in horses and riding, I'd been enrolled in the local Pony Club, which is the British system of horsemanship. Many an Olympic rider had their start coming up through the ranks of the Pony Club. I was already learning basic level dressage, practicing riding without stirrups or reins over cavalletti, and preparing for my first cross country jumping experience.

The Holloways learned of a retired hunter mare for sale by my new Pony Club instructor. We had seen the bay mare being ridden at a Pony Club event, and she seemed the kind of experienced older horse that could help bring a young rider along. I was extremely excited at the prospect. The day was set and we went to my instructor's home so I could try out the mare. When we arrived, she was already tacked up, and tied up outside the barn.

She was a tall, blood bay Standardbred mare, twelve years old. Her name was Tiggy.

With the help of a leg up I was on her, totally unafraid. She was responsive, but I noticed her gait was "off", it didn't feel right. My instructor assured me it was just that I wasn't used to her much longer stride, and the Holloways nodded in agreement, trusting this expert horsewoman and family friend. June wrote the check for $1,000 on the spot, and arrangements were made for the mare to be delivered later that week.

When the big day arrived, we all went out to the barn so I could greet our new arrival, delivered just a few hours earlier while I was at school. I had helped Snow prepare her stall with a deep bedding of sawdust, filling the manger with our own farm hay, and putting a treat of grain in her feed bin. I opened the stall door. The mare was standing at the back dozing. As I stepped into her stall, she awoke in a start and spun as fast as a freight train, ears pinned back, mouth open, teeth bared and came straight for me. Because I was so short, she missed her mark, and I stumbled back out the door trembling from head to foot. Tears rolled down my cheeks at this sudden and unexpected rejection and attempted assault - by a horse!

June and Snow were in shock. Here we were hosting children for the 4-H Hoof Beats Horsemanship Club, and they had purchased an attack horse! In fact, anytime anyone approached her stall door, the mare would charge with teeth bared. We immediately installed a web stall guard over her door and posted a sign: *Warning! This horse bites!* We soon learned a lot of this was an act. The mare was a retired Standardbred race horse, and no doubt had been abused at the track. A bucket with some grain would usually make it so you could snap on a lead rope, and once she was out of her stall, she was a gentle as a lamb.

A few days after her arrival, I saddled up Tiggy, using the mounting block to get on board, and rode her out to our little arena. At the walk all seemed fine. But when I asked her to trot, there was no doubt about it this time, the mare was dead lame. We immediately called our vet to examine her. He confirmed our worst fears; she had foundered recently, he said, pointing out the subtle rings on her hooves where the heat from laminitis had damaged them. She was permanently lame, could be used for light riding, walk and trot only on soft footing, or could be used as a brood mare. We all stood in stunned silence at the news. My Pony Club instructor had knowingly sold us a permanently lame and disabled horse and pocketed the $1,000!

I never would have the kind of mount that could take me to the levels of riding I aspired to, even when a very capable and experienced horse was offered on a free lease basis. When the owner, impressed with my riding, offered me the use of her horse as she was going off to college, June found a reason it wouldn't work. This horse had taken two riders to the top "A" ranking in Pony Club, and I was devastated when June turned down such a fantastic opportunity. There were limits to how far I was allowed to grow or succeed. June had her plans for me and our lives together. I was kept under tight reins, not realizing how masterfully I was being manipulated to assure I would never stray too far from her comfort zone and control.

The following summer, we hosted two Fresh Air Campers from New York City for two weeks. Children from low income families, many living in large, inner city apartment "projects", are matched with a host family to experience life outside the confines of the big city. The two brothers, Roy and Lee, were the first African American children I'd ever met. They'd never set foot outside of New York City. And so, I did my best to introduce them to the country life I loved. They were afraid of almost everything - bugs, the ponies, dogs, the dark and water. But soon they were playing and doing all the things I liked to do.

My biggest accomplishment during those two weeks was teaching the younger boy, Lee, how to hold his breath under water, and how to do the dog paddle. He arrived terrified of the water, and left proud of his ability to hold his breath longer than his older brother. We also picked and sold raspberries from our roadside stand, watched the best 4th of July fireworks ever, rode in the back of the pickup truck on errands to town, pretended we were cowboys, and played endless games of hide and seek. The two weeks of country life was transformational, and I felt a twinge of sadness, for my sake, and theirs, when they left. I wondered what would become of them and where their lives in New York City would lead.

Summer was also a time of hard work. I was Snow's helper for all major farm work. Our fields were primed for haying and after Snow mowed the fields; my job was to pull the rope on the dump rake, forming the windrows. When the hay was dry, I stood on top of the load tramping it down as it grew to a great mound towering over the truck cab. When we delivered it to the barn, I used a special rake to off load and fill the empty box stalls we used to store the hay for winter.

Haying was always the hottest days in early July. I would be red faced from the heat, and the need to wear jeans and long sleeved shirts to keep the prickly chaff at bay. We'd go in at noon, relishing glasses of iced tea and sandwiches June prepared in the air conditioned comfort she required to survive the dog days of summer. Haying was exhausting work, but I loved the sweet smell of freshly mown hay and watching the barn swallows swoop and dive all around us, feasting on insects. When the hay was all tucked away in the barn, the first snows came and we were feeding it to the horses, I was proud of my part in it all. Snow was too, and would proudly declare, "Yep, Deb, that's money in the bank. That hay is money in the bank."

During spring break, Snow would back the manure spreader into the barn, and my job was to clean out the sheep pens and horse stalls, that had been regularly layered with fresh bedding, but not mucked out. This was the old "Maine Way", allowing the manure to give off heat against the cold winter. But this kind of barn management ran counter to what I'd learned in Pony Club, and it created a sore point between Snow and me. He simply refused to allow us to have a manure pile. The manure would remain in the stalls until it was spread on the fields in the spring. I would fill several spreaders full of manure so strong it made my eyes water, before we'd finally get to the bare, damp floors. We'd spread those with lime and then at last, bed each sheep box and horse stall with a thick layer of fresh bedding.

Snow and I did regular runs to the local sawmill to pick up free loads of sawdust which we loaded and off loaded one shovel full at a time. Snow had built sides for the truck, so we could get three times as much in each load. In winter, there were many paths, doorways and gates in need of shoveling, and water to be hauled for the horses. I also had house chores, primarily vacuuming and dusting, two chores June loathed and saw no need to do as she had two able bodied helpers under her roof.

My life other than school revolved around the animals, the barn chores and being outside. I had no interest, and was not made to take interest, in cooking, sewing, home making or other "domestic" duties. In the barn with animals and outdoors is where I thrived. But June made sure my life and education were well rounded, introducing me to classical music, the theater, ballet, literature and art. These fed other aspects of my soul that had been thirsty for so long. I loved it all.

I was given art lessons in drawing, had beautiful art books from her collection to peruse and was taken periodically to art and science museums in Boston. When classical ballet performances were aired on public television, June would sometimes let me stay up late or come and wake me from my sleep to watch Rudolf Nureyev or Mikhail Baryshnikov dance in a stunning Swan Lake, or Nutcracker.

There was pop culture, too, as in those days television was a source of real entertainment. The three of us wedged into the small love seat in the sitting room, and watched the Beatles' U.S. debut on the Ed Sullivan Show. June was also a world news junkie, reading articles to me from the weekly *Newsweek Magazine* and tuning in to the television nightly news. Most evenings I ate my supper to the comforting voice of television news anchor, Walter Cronkite signing off with "And that's the way it is, Tuesday, June 15th, 1963."

I flourished under such tutelage. It was like giving food and water to someone who was starving. My education, exposure to arts and culture, and our farm life nourished me in every way, and would serve me all my life. Despite whatever disappointments and hurts life had in store for me, I would remain forever grateful for the doors June opened in my world.

My closest friends were school chums and neighbors, Lenny and Sally. Sally had pet flying squirrels she raised as abandoned youngsters. I spent many happy hours with her and her wonderful family at their resort campground on Mirror Lake just a mile up the road. Lenny and I shared many hours together out of doors at the farm or at his lakeside home, playing cards and chess when it rained, and teasing each other mercilessly.

But my friend Lenny lived in fear of his stern father, and I'd been witness to his cruelty more than once. One day, he made Lenny come to school the same morning both his beloved Collie dogs had fallen through the thin spring lake ice and drowned. Len sat in tears at his desk, while the other boys taunted him. I got up furious, and shoved one of the boys to the floor, sitting on top of him until he said he was sorry. I don't know where our teacher was at the time, but when she returned to the classroom, no one said a word about what I had done.

Then one November afternoon, during social studies class, the principal came into our fourth grade class room, wheeling a TV on a stand. Lenny, Sally and I, along with our entire class, sat in stunned silence, as footage of President Kennedy being shot flashed across the screen. And then the dreaded news confirmed by Walter Cronkite, "President Kennedy died at one o'clock, Central Standard Time. "

At home I had a scrap book filled with photos of Jaqueline Kennedy wearing beautiful gowns, arm in arm with her handsome husband, or riding alongside her daughter, Caroline on her pinto pony, Macaroni. Caroline was about my age, and it was exciting to feel a connection to the First Family through our shared love of horses. The news made me nauseous, and fearful. The President of the United States had been murdered. The world was not a safe place.....for any of us.

And before long, my own world would be turned upside down once more. One beautiful spring day just before Easter, I leapt off the school bus and there on the front lawn was a sign - *Real Estate for Sale.*

I couldn't believe it! I was devastated at the thought of once again losing my new friends, my new school where I'd settled in, hosting the 4-H Hoof Beats Horsemanship Club which I loved; leaving the farm

I'd explored every acre of, reveling in nature and all the seasons there. We had a large menagerie of animals now too...sheep, bantam hens, rabbits, the four horses and ponies, two dogs and cats...would they all be coming with us? Why were we moving again?! Weren't we happy here? Apparently not.

Chapter 11

Invisible Scars

*J*une chose her next location in Peterborough, based on the excellent public schools there. Soon we were preparing for another massive move, packing up all of June's many family heirlooms, thousands of books, and a huge barn full of Snow's tools, farm equipment, lumber, and so much more. Many of the animals would not accompany us to our smaller "estate".

Once again, I was leaving school friends and a place I had loved to explore riding my ponies, from the frog pond and sprawling pastures to swimming in the small cove on the lake. Lenny, Sally and other neighbor friends and I had skated on the pond and sledded on the hills in winter; we'd ridden the ponies together in the summer; and celebrated the end of the school year when our kindly bus driver treated us all to an ice cream at the local stand. The last day of school also signaled permission to go swimming for the first time, and we had rushed home to pull on our swim suits and meet up at either Sally or Lenny's beach front homes on the lake. Now, all too soon, my life and new friendships in Mirror Lake were to come undone. I felt some part of me was being swallowed up, as I stood powerless and afraid amidst the rapidly shifting sands of my life.

The move to Peterborough was traumatic. When the moving van arrived and the movers began off-loading the antiques, it was a devastating sight. Furniture had been packed without proper padding; large heavy pieces had been stacked on much more delicate ones. Fragile Sheraton and Chippendale furniture arrived scratched and gouged, with legs broken. The grandfather clock was delivered into the house with its glass clock face hanging open, its clock works banging around inside its beautifully detailed case. Barrels of Rose Medallion, Canton and Staffordshire china rattled like shells, broken to bits with improper packing. June sued the moving company for damages and got a paltry settlement of $2,000 which didn't cover the replacement cost of one single antique damaged in the move. She never had any of the furniture repaired, so we lived with the visible scars of that move on a daily basis.

I had no idea of the internal scars, patterns and beliefs that were forming inside of me, and how they would continue to deepen, shape and color my life for decades. And like those shattered tea cups, I was beginning to feel fragile and broken. Where was there any solid ground for me to stand on?

My core beliefs were being shaped by my life experiences. I longed for connection, roots and stability, and thought I had found that with the Holloways. Instead, I was repeatedly being torn from the places and people I loved, never allowed to really settle in anywhere for long. Beginning with chronic moving from place to place in and around Worcester during my early childhood, this was a pattern that would become ingrained in my life. By the time I was thirty, I could name thirty different places I had called "home" for at least a short time.

My world was being built on a foundation of shifting sands, and a home life predicated on my performing well in school, and "keeping up appearances". I was paraded in front of guests and relatives to show off how much June and Snow had done for me and how I was thriving under their generous (and expensive) tutelage and care. I was reminded often how much my education and life with the Holloways cost and how expensive it was to keep a roof over my head. These were the same messages I'd received living in poverty with my own mother. I would grow into adulthood with a great deal of shame around my own self-worth and face many challenges with money.

I was living a "privileged" life, yet a hole was growing in my soul; a sense of not "belonging" anywhere or to anyone who really loved me just for me. I adopted the belief I had to be "perfect" to be accepted and loved. Yet nothing I did was ever quite good enough in the eyes of those closest to me. I lived in fear that I would fail and be swallowed up once more by the nightmare of my past. Something wasn't right;

something just didn't click, despite all the external material blessings. In fact, material things were thrown my way often by June to "buy and keep me" along with her expectation of my endless gratitude for being "rescued". She had other expectations of me as well, which would be put to the test soon enough.

I couldn't name what was missing. But looking back, I can see it plainly. I simply wanted to be loved and to feel secure in that love; without the attachment of personal agendas and expectations to "perform" and make June or others look good. A deeply seated fear of failure, accompanied by an undercurrent of chronic anxiety would haunt me through childhood and well into adulthood. Only until I could heal issues to their core and restructure my belief systems would I find any relief. By now, I also had deeply ingrained, and largely unconscious beliefs that "to survive" I had to meet the needs and expectations of others, laying my own inner needs aside.

I was enrolled in the Peterborough public school mid-year. By now, I dreaded the entire feat of having to start not only in a new school, but in the middle of the term. To my surprise, I did make one classmate friend for what remained of the school year; a girl who like me, was an avid reader. For the new semester, our teacher started a bookworm growing around the class room, each segment of the worm a book a student had read. Margaret and I were head to head leaders for the most books read. At that time, I was the kind of reader who took a flashlight to bed to finish a book, as was my new friend. We continued our friendly reading rivalry, eventually tying for the number of books read, more than the rest of the class combined. And I adored our teacher for reading aloud to us after lunch time, and her book of choice -*The Black Stallion* by Walter Farley!

Margaret and I became friends outside of school as well. Only when I was invited to her home for dinner did I learn she was the daughter of the Governor! One day I accompanied Margaret and her mother to the Capitol Building in Concord. While her mother visited with her husband and colleagues over a cup of tea, we went roaming the halls of the New Hampshire Capitol, exploring secret hiding places Margaret knew about. But another friendship would be short lived, as behind the scenes, June was making other plans for my education, yet to be revealed.

That spring, Snow and I began watching Lady closely. She was due to give foal to a Half Arabian sired by Radsun during their summer pasturing at the farm in Mirror Lake. I was so excited, watching her belly swell, waiting for the telltale signs of the "softening of the bones" around her tail making way for the birth of the foal, and finally the swelling of her milk bag and waxing of her teats.

When the time seemed close at hand, Snow and I took turns checking on her every few hours. How the school days dragged on until I could get home and run to the barn to see if she had foaled! Finally, one evening during supper, I jumped up from the table. I just knew she was having the foal. And sure enough, Lady was still standing, but the two front legs of the foal were protruding from beneath her tail. I dashed back to the house to get Snow, and we watched as within the next half hour, a beautiful bay filly with a white star was born.

That summer I trained Dolly how to be haltered and led; how to leave her mother for periods of time in preparation for the day she would be weaned, to soften the often traumatic experience for mare and foal. I proudly showed them off to neighbor children, until one day disaster struck.

A boy and girl lived next door. I didn't really like them, but they insisted on seeing Lady and her filly. While they were visiting, the boy asked if he could get up on Lady. I didn't see why not. I had her on a lead line, and could lead him around the little field. I gave him a leg up, but instead of swinging his leg over her back, he simply slid across Lady's back, landing in a heap on the ground beside her. He cried out that he'd hurt his arm and got up holding it. Then he and his sister ran home to tell their parents.

It wasn't long before his father called our house in a rage, threatening to sue us for negligence. Soon after, the papers for the lawsuit arrived and a court date was set. I was living in terror of what might happen. When news of the threat reached our house, I was sent to my room. I could hear Snow and June speaking in hushed tones, and I feared that I'd be sent back to Worcester, or worse, to live in a foster home for all the trouble I caused. It turned out the family had such a long track record of law suits, it was practically a source of supplementary income. Nevertheless, we were sued for having an "attractive nuisance" on our property. The fallout from this was to follow soon enough.

We now had a small family of horses and I had begun to ride Radsun; he was coming three years old and a stallion. Although he was gentle, stallions are not considered reliable mounts for children, as a mare in season can very quickly alter a stallion's otherwise demure behavior. So June made arrangements to have him gelded and trained in exchange for a couple of her grandfather's antique carriages. It wasn't until I came home from school one day, that I learned the rest of the bargain, one that rid us of any and all unwanted "nuisances".

I walked up the driveway from the school bus, just as the man was closing the ramp on the trailer. Inside, were Lady, her un-weaned filly and Cindy. I stood frozen in time, watching the back of the trailer, and another piece of my heart, roll further and further away, until they disappeared down the road and out of sight.

It seemed like the only thing I could count on in my life was more uncertainty, upheaval and loss; and all of it beyond my control or comprehension. My nightmares of being suffocated returned, along with those of riding helplessly in a car as it careened down the road until it missed a turn and soared over a cliff. Though I'd try desperately to wake myself up, I would be in the car until it exploded, and then I'd be hovering over the scene wondering how I'd get home again. Versions of this nightmare haunted my sleep for decades.

June was keeping her commitment to give me a good education, and set her next plan into action. I was withdrawn from Peterborough public school and enrolled the next fall in a small private day school in Chelmsford, Massachusetts, two hours away. The school week schedule was an ordeal especially as winter set in … up at five, leave at six, drive one hour to the school bus stop; depart there at seven, arriving at school by eight o'clock. Then I'd repeat the same process in reverse each afternoon, arriving home after five p.m., have supper and then two or more hours of homework.

Poor Snowie was the designated chauffer morning and evening in addition to bringing June breakfast in bed along with endless cups of tea each morning, farm chores, and doing all the property maintenance. In fact, June never saw me off to school as she didn't have her first cup of tea in bed until 9 a.m. But she made sure plans were in place, leaving me my breakfast and lunch all made. She knew I was in good keeping with the man who really was the glue that held our lives together, Snow. But since June held the purse strings and only gave Snow enough money for gas and sundries, she held all the power and control. Snow and I were pawns on the chessboard of her life, never consulted about decisions large or small that impacted us greatly.

After half a year of this routine had taken its toll on both Snow and me, another plan was devised. June had some church friends who lived close to one of the school bus stops, about an hour and a half from Peterborough, and only a 30 minute bus ride to school. Starting the next semester, I would spend the entire school week with this church friend, Mrs. Kurwin, her elderly mother and two teenage daughters. They had a small spare room that I could use as my own.

I didn't see why I couldn't just go to the nearby school like before. Peterborough being a wealthy community had excellent schools. But June wanted me enrolled in a private school like those she had attended. The family was nice enough, but I missed my animals, coming home to my own family such as it was, and sleeping in my own room. The little house sat by a busy numbered route, had a small yard with a lone apple tree, and there was absolutely nothing for me to do besides the tons of homework I had each night.

Mrs. Kurwin was an excellent cook, and so I took comfort in food. But it did nothing to ease my acute loneliness and feeling of not "belonging" anywhere. I managed to continue to be on the honor roll in school and was often up until midnight just to complete the massive homework assignments. My nightmares returned, but I had no one I could talk to about my night terrors, anxiety and underlying fear that was beginning to take over my mind, heart and spirit. I knew that I had to "perform" well to keep my place with the Holloways. I always felt if I failed in any way I would be sent away, mostly likely back to where I came from, and that I dreaded most of all.

On Fridays, June and Snow would make the drive down to Chelmsford to pick me up. What a welcome relief to be reunited! We had dearly missed each other during the school week. We'd get an ice cream to celebrate the weekend and drive home with June's little Dachshund riding shotgun upfront. What a relief to be back with the animals, in my lovely room, and feeling safe. But now, I lived in the secret dread of what unexpected event would next overturn my life.

One thing was for certain, I didn't know anyone whose childhood looked anything like mine. And no one knew the kind of life I'd had in Worcester. My classmates thought I was living with my grandparents, and asked where my parents were. Every time a "regular mom and dad" came to pick up their children after school, I felt that hole open in my soul, and shame that my own mother and father had not wanted me. Unlike all the children I knew, I had no brothers or sisters to accompany me on this journey. And since June had secured an unlisted phone number as soon as the adoption was legal, there was no contact with any of my Worcester relatives either.

It was only my aunt I really missed, as she was the only adult who had really "just loved me". She was the only relative who cared enough to keep searching for me after our move from Amherst. I would be an adult before I'd see her again. As for my mother, once my adoption was final, I never saw or heard from her again.

June had also been quietly discarding all mail addressed to me from Worcester relatives to make sure the divide between us remained permanent. Years later, I would learn that my Aunt Dorothy had sent me many packages, some that would have made me a "rock star" among my classmates and friends. Her employer in Worcester had many federal contracts, including some with NASA. Dorothy worked on the Gemini projects, the earliest manned space missions. She was a patent maker and glove specialist. She assisted in the design and construction of the astronaut's life-saving space suits, and designed, crafted and fitted the complex, three layered gloves for each astronaut.

Dorothy was sent to Cape Canaveral several times to personally measure and fit astronauts "Gus" Grissom John Young, and others with the gloves they would wear during their several hour, to several day orbits around the earth. These flights were the prelude to man's first walk on the moon, just a few years later. During her time working with NASA, my Aunt Dorothy was gifted with autographed photos, samples of "space food", and other NASA and Gemini memorabilia. She had mailed it all to me, but I would never receive any of it, or enjoy the thrill of sharing it with my classmates and friends. June had thrown everything in the trash, after opening each package to satisfy her own curiosity. But she certainly wasn't going to be upstaged by one of my Worcester relatives!

Life with June and Snow had been a gift of grace, yes. But as the months went by, it was clear, that darker forces were also at work in our lives. And more and more I began to feel like a "freak"; someone who really didn't fit in or belong anywhere. I was often picked on at school, not only for always being the "new kid in class", but for the homemade or hand me down outfits June insisted I wear, along with "responsible" brown tie leather shoes, and the dreaded plaid book bag. If only kids weren't so cruel, and I didn't want so desperately to fit in somewhere.

It was the animals and nature that gave me the solace, companionship and affection I craved. Without their presence, I would have slipped much deeper into the gaping hole that was growing in my soul. No one noticed anything different about me, other than I'd grown quite chubby on Mrs. Kurwin's home cooking. On the outside, I was still obsessed with anything to do with horses. I remained an honor roll student and a helpful and obedient child. It was on the inside that I was changing, feeling bouts of overwhelming anxiety, depression, and desperate loneliness.

I reveled in the times we hosted a cookout or other get-togethers that brought friends or cousins together. I would hide with the guest children, and we'd let our parents call for us until the brink of punishment, just for a few more minutes of companionable bliss. These children, had two parents who loved them, as well as grandparents and siblings. They had the stability of a home and had attended the same school with their friends for years. I could only imagine what that kind of life would be like; to know you were loved and wanted, where you belonged, and that the ground under your feet was solid….not quick sand ready to swallow you up at any moment.

In the ten short years I lived with the Holloways, we lived in seven different homes and moved six times; I attended seven different schools and two colleges. They moved several more times, well into their eighties, in June's effort to quell whatever demons she was battling. These patterns would get imprinted on me as well, and no place would feel like home for very long.

When we have experienced a great loss or chronic trauma, it can seem that we are being punished by God, by Spirit, by Life. We can feel singled out as being unlovable. For some of us, because of our life experiences, especially as children, we may have internalized the beliefs that we are unworthy and deserving of punishment. We can become so overly responsible we even blame ourselves when things "go wrong" within our families or in our lives. Yet, sometimes things "go wrong" so we can have a fresh start and a new direction.

Our internal self-talk, coming from our ego mind, can lead us down a dark road that is not at all what our Soul-Spirit is seeking. The ego-mind fears the unknown, and creates illusions to distract us and keep us from wandering too far from what is familiar, even if it is painful. Yet, our soul seeks expansion, awakening and the Light of Unconditional Love. Our soul remembers. It strives tirelessly to help us wake up and find our way home.   - Debra Lightheart

Chapter 12

Mind Games

*P*uberty was to launch a wave of changes and not just the biological ones. Something about my growing into adolescence triggered June's fears and her deepening need for control. It also brought out a much darker side than I'd seen at work before, one that was cruel and bent on humiliation. At its worst, it became a "crazy making" nightmare, which during the early stages of my healing journey, my outspoken therapist referred to as "mind fuck".

The onset of my monthly period and bodily changes marked the beginning of further shame and humiliation not only at home, but at school. In gym class I was teased mercilessly, as I was still not wearing a bra. In class or in the halls, girls would run their fingers down my back, and hoot and holler in front of the boys, "Debbie's not wearing a bra!"

At thirteen, I was not tuned in to my changing body other than feeling more and more shame. I came home in tears, sharing my humiliation with my "mother" and begging that I be allowed to buy my first bra. Instead, she took all my undershirts and sewed a wide piece of elastic across the back, so when the girls taunted me they'd be fooled into thinking I was wearing a bra. Oh, to keep me from growing up at any price! But you could as soon hold back the tide, as the surge of teenage hormones.

Eventually, when the truth could no longer be ignored, she gave Snow a wad of cash and told him to take me shopping for a bra. We were both too embarrassed for words, as he hid out in the men's clothing aisle, and I shamefully asked the sales clerk for assistance with purchasing a bra. June herself had given up wearing bras years earlier, long before the women's movement, for reasons of comfort. June's appearance was a further source of embarrassment to me as a teenager, especially at school functions. But nothing could compare to the humiliation she would heap on me the night of the science fair.

I came home from school that day anxious about the upcoming parent's night and science fair exhibition. The truth was that I'd had no interest or ambition for this assignment. I did an uninspired project on growing plants in different kinds of light. I was just hoping for a grade that wouldn't ruin my overall average. I didn't even have much prepared to say about it. I just couldn't seem to muster any enthusiasm. I was dreading the evening, and would be glad to have it behind me.

After supper, as I was about to go upstairs and change into the outfit I'd picked out to wear, June summoned me into the living room. She had a beach towel draped over her arm, and she was in the kind of elated state I now recognized as trouble.

"I've made something for you to wear tonight", she beamed, holding up the towel. It was a hideous lime green and blue. She'd sewn the edges together into a dress, leaving openings for over the head, two sleeveless armholes with the fringe forming the hem.

"Now go on upstairs, and put it on. We don't have much time before we leave."

"I can't wear that to the science fair", I protested."

"Yes, you can, and you will," she persisted.

"I won't wear it! You can't make me wear it to the science fair tonight! I'll wear it another time", I lied. I wouldn't be caught dead wearing that hideous thing.

"You'll go put this on right now, or we'll stay home, and you'll get an F for your project. How does that sound?"

I was shocked into silence, then angry tears.

"I hate you!" I yelled as I grabbed the dress from her and fled upstairs.

The only shoes to choose from were my "respectable" brown leather ones, or sneakers. I chose the sneakers. I looked in the mirror, and began to sob. By now, I already had a shameful view of my body. The extra fifteen pounds I carried on my 5'2" frame were torture. And the handmade clothes June made for me were another source of ridicule from my fellow classmates, who shopped for fashionable clothes at high end department stores. June was in one of her manic "highs" savoring every moment of what soon would be my public humiliation. To make matters worse, it was a dreadfully hot and humid evening, so there was no way to cover up. The towel dress hung heavy and hot, causing me to perspire, adding to my overwhelming shame and embarrassment.

We arrived at my school and found my science class. I stood dumbly by my dreary exhibit, unable to hide my shame and humiliation, as one leering parent and smirking classmate after another passed by. My teacher stopped momentarily in his tracks, and then simply passed us by, sparing me further embarrassment. I was mortified, and didn't see how I could face my classmates and teachers the next day. I dreaded what would be fodder for more jokes and pranks for weeks to come. I rode home in silent shame and disgust. To my relief and surprise, at school the next day, and the next, not one word was spoken about my attire for the science fair. It was never mentioned. For once, even my classmates recognized there was a line even they would not cross.

But still, I was the target of bullying. One day, as I was leaving the locker room to go out for our field hockey practice, the only other girl in the room put her foot up across the doorway so I couldn't go out. She leaned against the wall with her foot on the tall grey metal locker blocking my path with an "I dare you" smirk. I pushed to get through her barrier, and she pushed even harder on the locker, toppling it over, to our shock. As it was falling I lurched forward past her brushing the sharp metal corner as I passed. When I looked down at my leg, I had a gapping six inch wound ripped open along the outside of my knee. The girl took one look, turned white as a sheet, and ran to get our gym teacher.

Miss Dyer drove me to the emergency room of the small local hospital and I was wheeled from the car inside. To our dismay, there was no doctor on duty to stitch me up. I hobbled back to the car on the arm of my teacher, and she drove me to a local physician. As he disinfected my wound I could smell liquor on his breath. The gaping cut had begun to swell. He hastily stitched up the nasty wound noting, "You're lucky. You came within a whisker of cutting an artery."

I was driven back to school by my gym teacher, attended my last class of the day and took the bus home as usual. Within two days I was ill with a high fever, as the wound had become infected. My leg throbbed unmercifully, and I was put on antibiotics. The ragged gash had been roughly stitched together, and when finally healed, left a long and ugly scar from my knee cap to the top of my calf. My classmate and her parents were holding their breath, expecting to get sued. To my knowledge, June never even contacted the parents, and no apology was ever offered. My stoic treatment of the whole event, and the horrible looking wound requiring sixteen stitches, earned me respect by my peers. Finally, the taunting ceased.

Our fifth move, to be closer to this school I was now attending, landed us on a spectacular three hundred acre homestead in Goffstown, New Hampshire. It featured a large three story, center chimney colonial, a huge barn and workshop. It was located on a dead end road, perched on a hill with mountain views overlooking rolling fields and a pond. An enormous horse chestnut tree grew outside the window of my bedroom, which faced the glorious western sunsets. There were endless places to ride, explore and commune with nature. I could easily see living the rest of my life in this nature's paradise.

Here my deep love of nature was nourished on a daily basis. My creative expression found room to flourish in art, music, and poetry. My "descriptive essay" on environmental pollution was published in the New Hampshire Audubon Journal when I was fifteen. I walked in the first Earth Day celebration. I carried within me a deep love of the land, animals, and the Earth. I was very troubled by the destruction of our wild places and the wanton slaughter of wild animals, as I viewed them as sacred. Despite the emotional turmoil in my outer world, I was already tapping into much older and deeper wisdom within my being.

I was now in my second year of private school in Manchester. We were active members of the Unitarian Church, where I sang in the children's choir and participated in LRY (Liberal Religious Youth) activities. The UU church had always been a place of spiritual and intellectual nourishment for me, introducing me early on to the Transcendentalists including Henry David Thoreau and Ralph Waldo Emerson, whose love of nature had resonated with me from the start. The church provided opportunities for me to gain confidence in public speaking, creating ceremony, and performing musically. It was one of the few places I could relax, be me and be accepted and celebrated for who I was…no strings attached.

My summer weekends were still devoted to Pony Club rallies, horse shows and three phase eventing. Radsun, though not ideally suited for some of the tasks asked of him, proved versatile and excelled in an array of equine pursuits. Three phase eventing was by far the most challenging test of our abilities. Our dressage test, riding a series of prescribed patterns and transitions to demonstrate the horse's balance, suppleness, precision and responsiveness was often among the highest scores. As we gained confidence, we were galloping over rugged terrain and jumping solid three foot cross country fences and obstacles, and navigating the fast, tricky stadium jumping courses with tight turns and combinations designed to cause a horse to "drop a rail" at the slightest touch, costing precious points. Neither one of us excelled at "jumping", but we crossed through our fears together forming a bond of trust. The little gelding gave me all he had as long as we were together. Neither of us knew that our future endeavors together would be short lived.

Snow seemed happy enough to haul us to these equine events, but I was mostly on my own once we arrived. He might watch for a while, but if I wasn't winning first place, or if we made mistakes, he'd walk away, shaking his head, disgusted. Usually, he spent the afternoon listening to Red Sox baseball on the radio or napping in the truck. I knew he was proud of my accomplishments, but he wasn't really able to offer the kind of support I craved. The other competitors had a whole cheering section coaching from the sideline, which wasn't "allowed", and when they won a ribbon, or to comfort them or offer encouragement when they didn't. Nevertheless, what self-confidence and pride I did have came in large measure from my years engaged in the equestrian arts.

I finished out my second year at the small private day school finally an insider and making some friends, although due to our isolated location, I never saw them outside of school. And there was one more thing. I had developed an obsessive crush on one of my teachers. He was our very charismatic and passionate English teacher. I excelled in his class, and he read one of my creative writing essays to close out the school year. I was so taken with him, June went to visit him at school, and invited he and his wife to come visit us at the farm. Nevertheless, my crush lasted the summer and I ached until the school year would resume. My "obsession" with unavailable men would become a pattern that would cause me great emotional anguish and prove very difficult to heal.

As June's moods darkened more often, my only escape was riding to the far reaches of the property to soothe my fraying spirit with the comfort of horses and nature. Little did I know, she was drafting up yet another set of plans for my life. She learned from the public school principal that I could graduate a year early by simply adding the one "required" senior course to my curriculum. June waited until summer break was nearly over to inform me I would not be returning to Derryfield for my junior year. She had already enrolled me in our small town's public school, with its worn text books, and even more worn out teachers.

I breezed along, as there was little homework, and my studies had already taken me well beyond the curriculum offered. Mid-terms came with some disappointing news for June. The school board had overruled the principal's decision, and would not let me graduate early, even though I was completing the one extra credit required and was an Honor Roll student. This called for a new plan of action.

So mid-year, of what was now to be my senior year of high school, I was sent to live with our cousins who lived in another school district, which had definitely agreed to allow me to graduate one year early, at the age of sixteen. Meanwhile, June had secretly submitted "my" application to Dartmouth College, which had recently announced it was accepting women. I can only imagine what "my essay" said about why I wanted to attend Dartmouth! Perhaps, if she'd allowed ME to complete the application, I would have been admitted, but we'll never know.

My photo in the Senior Year Book of my new high school was embarrassing. I'm wearing a June-made mid-calf length, navy blue corduroy jumper, puff sleeved blouse, and sneakers. Since I didn't yet drive and had no money of my own to spend, most of my clothing options were still those of the eight year old child June wished I still was. Yet, at the same time, I was being rushed to finish high school while nearly two years younger than my classmates, and missing out on all the non-academic activities. But the biggest adjustment was leaving the comfort of a small school where I knew nearly all the students, to join a regional high school, where our senior class alone had five hundred students...and I didn't know a single one.

I completed my senior year living with my cousin Jane's parents during the school week, coming home on weekends. Jane and her brother were off at college themselves now, so after eating dinner, I'd retreat to her bedroom with its canopy bed and desk to do my homework and practice folksongs on her abandoned guitar. I missed my cousin and the happy times we'd shared and I was feeling more and more lonely and adrift in my life.

When graduation day was approaching, I invited Malcolm and Louise to attend, which I thought was proper considering they were providing me room and board at June's request and expense. I assumed June would be pleased to have them join us, especially as

Mac was a big personality and always the life of the party. I couldn't have been more mistaken.

When I mentioned to June I had invited Mac and Louse, she flew into a rage.

"How dare you invite them before inviting Snowie and me to your high school graduation, after all we've done for you?!!" She was livid and declared she would not attend my graduation.

I protested, "Of course you're invited! You're my parents for heaven's sake! I can have up to six guests!" She would hear none of it, and for days went about slamming the door in my face whenever I appeared, even locking me out of the house for hours at a time.

Later, when she confronted me with her own versions of "the graduation story" of what happened and when, I told her I had proof of what transpired recorded in my diary.

Now she became a mad woman and insisted, "You'll not go on living under this roof keeping such lies! You'll burn that filthy diary and your lies with it! Go upstairs right this minute and bring it down here!"

"Mother" was driving me mad with her wild accusations and bizarre behaviors. I furiously stomped upstairs to my desk and found my red leather bound diary with its brass clasp she'd given me the prior Christmas. I'd lost the key, but had never used it anyway. Being a chilly spring evening, June had a fire burning in the enormous central fireplace. I flew down the stairs in a teenage rage, flinging my diary into the fire. I retreated back upstairs to my room, crying with anger and heartbreak. After all the hoops I'd jumped through to complete school on June's terms, she was now threatening to not even attend my graduation!

In a little while, I stopped sobbing to grab some Kleenex and blow my nose. I could hear June's monotone voice coming up through the open heat vent in the floor. It couldn't be! It simply couldn't be!

I raced downstairs to find June reading my diary out loud to Snow. She had quickly retrieved my hastily tossed journal from the flames, and other than a little charring on the thick cover, it was perfectly intact. And there she sat, reading aloud my most private thoughts, feelings, and aspirations. Caught in the act of such a deceitful and despicable act, it was the only time I saw her look sheepish over anything she did. Snow, as always, was the obliging, totally co-dependent victim of his circumstances. I never really blamed him for his part in my abuse; I knew his heart was never in it, and what hell he'd have paid for not complying with her wishes.

I flew into an uncontrolled rage, yelling at the top of my lungs, "You fucking bitch! You fucking bitch!" I grabbed the journal from her, my hands trembling, as I tore the pages from my diary, throwing them onto the fire and making sure they were burned to ash, shaking and sobbing the entire time. Then I ran outside, slamming the door as hard as I could.

The next day I awoke in searing emotional pain that was seeking relief at any cost. This feeling had been growing in me for some time, but today it was excruciating. While Snow was serving June her breakfast in bed, I went to his medicine cabinet to seek relief. All I found was half a bottle of aspirin, and his razor blades. I got a glass of water and downed all the aspirin but they did nothing to dull my agonizing emotional pain. I put a razor blade in my pocket and headed up across the two large hay fields, tears streaming down my face, ignoring all the beauty of nature that for so long had been my comfort and solace. I was beyond comfort now. Nothing in this world could ease the pain in my heart and soul, or my self-loathing.

When I reached the stone wall over the hill at the far side of the last field, I climbed over it and sat facing into the dark tangle of woods, far out of sight and sound. I sat there crying for a long time, my mind filled with dark thoughts. Finally, I took the razor blade from my pocket, and slowly drew the first cut across my wrist.

Blood oozed to the surface, but I had not cut deeply enough to do any real damage. For the entire afternoon, I tried to summon the courage to make the one deep cut it would take to end my misery and the misery I caused others, once and for all. By day's end, I had bloody scratches up and down the inside of both wrists and arms. Each time I would bring the razor to my flesh, I felt this overwhelming presence, this inner and outer force that was crying out, "Stop! Don't do this! Don't do this! Don't do this!" The truth is, I didn't want to die. But I desperately wanted an end to my excruciating emotional pain.

My angels and protectors were with me that day, as I came within a few millimeters of taking my own life. I spent the entire day and night curled up against the backside of the stone wall. When I finally returned to the house in the wee hours of morning, to my surprise, "Mother" was dozing on the couch in the living room. She took one look at my arms, and a strange look came over her face as she said, "I didn't think you'd have the guts to do it. You kept me up all night for no good reason."

When company arrived that weekend she flaunted what I'd done, noting how my ungrateful behavior had caused her to have spells of high blood pressure and trips to the doctor. Meanwhile, I was never taken to see a counselor or therapist. Instead, June announced that since I enjoyed drama so much, she'd enrolled me in the summer theater internship program at the University of New Hampshire. I would be spending my entire summer in college, having just graduated high school with honors and a college scholarship at sixteen.

In a bizarre way, this probably was the best solution. It meant I would be away from June's crazy making behaviors, though totally out of my league in terms of the age and sophistication of the seasoned actors enrolled in the program. June had pulled some strings for sure since I had no formal theater or acting experience besides a school play in seventh grade. I was incredibly shy, insecure, had low self-esteem and little stage presence.

Yet, I reveled in the talents of those around me and blossomed over the summer, performing an original mime piece with a partner in the public student performance. We produced four plays that summer to sold-out UNH Summer Theater audiences. I was prop girl for Puck in *A Midsummer Night's Dream*; I ran the follow spot light on Don Quixote for every performance of *Man of La Mancha*; was understudy to a lead actress in *The Importance of Being Ernest,* and helped with publicity for the ground breaking play, *The Boys in the Band.* Some of my fellow actors went on to land roles in television series and Broadway plays.

While I thought I also heard the call to be a thespian, it really was not in my comfort zone to be on stage; nor was I into the pervasive free-wheeling sex and drugs off stage. What could well have launched my exploration of both, through some miracle, did not. I never had any interest in alcohol or recreational drugs, which severely limited making friends in my teen and college years. As far as dating or sex, while well informed, I still had no idea exactly how much my early childhood experiences would impact me as I crossed into those waters.

In an unexpected surprise acknowledgement of my early graduation and college start, June announced one day she was sending me and her eldest granddaughter on a ten day trip to Paris. Elizabeth had grown up in the suburbs of Boston, so June felt confident we could manage on our own at sixteen and seventeen. June had made reservations for us at an old hotel near the Paris Opera House. She herself had spent several summers abroad, making numerous crossings of the Atlantic by steam ship, and considered a European excursion essential to one's education.

Each morning, my "cousin" and I enjoyed our complimentary continental breakfast of café au lait with our brioche and croissant. Then we set about being American tourists. My first impressions of Paris were somewhat shocking to me. My tall, blond "cousin" and I were constantly harassed by Frenchmen and repeatedly had our bottoms pinched as a manner of course! When not fending off handsome and horny Frenchmen, who apparently saw us as "easy and loose" American women, we sampled French food, largely from street vendors and cafés. We drank strong coffee in the bohemian West Bank arts district, ate escargot, (requesting to keep the snail shells, to the delight of the waiters), visited the flower vendors in the park, cruised the River Seine and enjoyed views from the top of the Eiffel Tower. We sat in the moonlight on the steps of Sacré Coeur and devoted an entire day to viewing the great works of art in the Louvre.

Of all the splendid sights to see during our short stay, Notre Dame Cathedral left the deepest impression on me: her soaring arched ceilings, flying buttresses, and enormous stained glass rose windows, the scale of it all, and incomparable artistry and craftsmanship. The sacred feeling of the place touched something deep within, and moved me to tears. On our last evening as Americans in Paris, we sipped cappuccinos in a café on Avenue des Champs Elysée, each of us hoping to keep the magic alive when we returned to our disjointed lives in New England.

Those souls that converge to form family systems, especially those with great dysfunction, are drawn together by karmic connections and patterns seeking resolution. Old soul wounds and dramas will be triggered again and again until there is an opening in consciousness, a willingness within the heart and soul to disengage, step back and find a path toward healing.

Many who are deeply wounded project their shadow onto others, making those around them the source of their suffering. Until one can find the courage to face their own pain and accept responsibility for their own healing, they will remain caught in the web of suffering and the illusion of being helpless and powerless. Often these souls look outside themselves for this power by seeking to manipulate and control others to fill their own internal void and temporarily quell their own suffering.

Often, such patterns are inherited and passed from generation to generation. Yet, each of us has the capacity to transform suffering into healing, wisdom and grace. It may take many lifetimes before our wisdom flowers forth to restore balance and harmony. Yet every soul has the urgent longing and the capacity to heal and to shine its Light brightly in the world. For this is our true mission in life....to heal our souls, activate its power and shine our Light! — Debra LightHeart

Chapter 13

The Final Blow

I lived with the Holloways through two more excruciating moves, as June sold off the farm equipment, and all the horses but Radsun. Snow's way of life was now put on the shelf as June feared for his age and health and wanted to be sure he'd be able to take care of her needs. She downsized two more times, donating many of her family heirlooms to museums, historical societies or giving them to wealthy members of her family so they would continue to be passed on to future generations.

By the time we landed together in Henniker, New Hampshire, June spent much of her time morose and withdrawn. She and Snow were now in their mid-seventies, and June focused more and more of her fearful thoughts of failing health, and how she could keep me close to home. She tried guilt, anger, the silent treatment. She tried to lure me with promises of a secure financial future one day and threats of disowning me the next. Her manipulative and outright deceitful behaviors only drove me further and further away, and continued to confuse and upset me at every turn. While I deeply loved and cared for Snow and June, living day in day out with her behaviors and mood swings, was driving me toward the same abyss I had approached once before.

One day, following a bitter argument when she shoved me into a corner yelling into my face, I knew it was make or break time. When June and Snow went out that afternoon, I drove to the home of a professional couple who'd been former neighbors. I sought out the comfort, safety and wisdom of their counsel. When I phoned home that evening, Snow answered. As soon as we began to speak, I heard June in the background yelling her instructions to Snow.

"Tell her not to come back here again! Tell her not to come back here again!

"Mother says not to come back here again," Snow echoed in a hollow and downcast tone. End of conversation. I hung up the phone in tears and disbelief.

Within ten days, June rid herself of all visible reminders of me.

Radsun was given to the neighbor of one of my closest and only long-time friends; my clothes and personal belongings were given to my cousin Jane and her family. I came out from college class one day to find "my" car, registered in June's name, being towed away, having been reported as a stolen vehicle. Next, the police arrived at the front door of my friends, where I'd sought refuge, to claim my little dog as hers. A few days later, an envelope arrived in the mail. Inside was stationary inscribed *"A little note from June...."* detailing the steps she'd been forced to take since "I'd abandoned her and dear old Snowie," adding that she'd had the little dog, Lucy, and my cat, William, put to sleep.

I was devastated, heartbroken and outraged that June would extend her punishment toward innocent animals. I was beside myself with grief, anger and fear. I never heard from friends or family to whom she had bestowed my belongings, and Radsun (also registered in her name, so not legally mine). They had apparently bought her "poor me" story, lock stock and barrel. June had effectively not only cut me out of her life, but the lives of the few other people in my support system by weaving them into her web as skillfully as the spider snags the fly.

I had just turned nineteen a few weeks earlier. Without a car or source of income, the first thing I did was drop out of college and look for a job. June eventually signed the car over to me, and made a brief attempt at reconciliation. At great expense, she purchased a double wide mobile home and had it situated in Radsun's former pasture. She paid for a paved driveway, hook up of utilities, and expected me to move right in. I had no intention of doing any such thing. There were several reasons this was not going to work, the most obvious one being the Henniker property was for sale.

By now, I was too wounded to be anywhere near June on a regular basis, let alone live with her. My very first job was factory assembly line work, which I did not excel at and I was soon fired. It did not elude me how closely this reenacted the path of my own mother back in Worcester. I soon landed a retail job and later an administrative job, and began as best I could to make my way in the world. The boyfriend I had met in the little public high school made contact with me and in need of something solid to anchor my life to, I married him when I was just twenty one. June continued to throw as many curves my way as she could, as despite it all, I tried to remain a good daughter, just not one living under her roof.

When June learned of my engagement, she filed a court order to have the furniture I had in my apartment returned. This was furniture that had been in the Henniker house when she purchased it, not family heirlooms. This was simply an act of spite. When she tried to take over the wedding plans, my soon to be husband told her off rudely on the phone and hung up on her. A few days later, my wedding gift from her, engraved sterling flatware, arrived via UPS. She and Snow boycotted the wedding, and my college graduation two years later. For several years, she rejected all my attempts at contact, returning letters and packages unopened, and refusing all phone calls.

But as aging raised more of her fears of being alone, we made one more attempt at a shared life. My husband and I moved into the ell of her latest purchase, another antique cape with a small barn, back in

Amherst. I knew my husband went along with it as he saw the potential for money coming his way thru the arrangement. It was my last ditch effort to be the grateful, responsible grown adult daughter. We paid the going rate of monthly rent to live in the ell and were June's "gophers", running errands, doing small repairs, maintenance and basic landscaping.

Every evening after work, I was expected to pay a visit, which June would drag out for over two hours if she could. I had two horses at the time, and Snow delighted in having me close by again, along with the horses. And for the first time, I helped him plant a vegetable garden. June saw the fondness between us and was jealous.

Nothing my husband and I did for June, or the place, was ever enough, and she played sick, manipulative games just for fun. My husband, whom she had shunned for several years, was now her "darling". On my birthday, she invited him to join her and Snow for a fall road trip and luncheon out. To my dismay, my husband gladly took the day off from work to oblige her, while I went to work as usual. When they returned, June was elated as she tossed my hastily wrapped gift on the table. Inside were a half empty package of file folders and a box of elastics. One of us was surely losing our mind, if not both.

Her other "game" was to tell any visitor, or complete stranger, how she had no family to leave her home and belongings to, and how this troubled her greatly. She'd set the bait for her unsuspecting victims, hooking them with her sad stories and dangling false hopes in front of them. When she tired of her game, she'd cut them out of her life, until the next unsuspecting candidate appeared.

One day, a total stranger appeared at our door and charmed his way into our living room. I knew the cat and mouse game had begun. He had a very convincing tale to tell set against her tale of woes. He was very supportive of June's need to distance herself from her selfish and neglectful adopted daughter.

He claimed he was a distant relative of Snow's and, by the end of the afternoon, June instructed Snow to load up his few precious belongings into the back of this man's truck. I watched as his two remaining beautiful hand crafted schooners, boxes of his priceless sets of antique planes and other valuable tools were loaded until the truck was jammed full. The man drove away and was never seen or heard from again.

"That bitch!" I was furious, at her lies, her schemes, and her total disrespect for Snow who had been her faithful husband, companion, servant, and property caretaker all these years. And I was deeply sad for myself. The only thing I had really wanted to have in my home, someday, was one of Snow's beautiful handmade ships. June knew exactly what she was doing. While she'd already made it known to me on several occasions she had written me out of her will, she was also making sure Snow would have nothing to leave me or anyone else in his life either.

Previously, June had blindly entrusted a financial advisor to invest her money. She was "taken" with him, and began to give him family heirlooms. She'd even bestowed one of our young horses to his family, though they were entirely unequipped with the knowledge or the facilities to care for a horse. It broke my heart to see this sensitive and beautiful animal left in the hands of novices.

It took a few years, but by constantly buying and selling June's stocks, this trusted financial advisor depleted one third of June's capital and interest, her only source of income. Nothing could be done after the fact, and the broker received a mere slap on his wrist, and continued business as usual.

June preferred charlatans to her own family – a daughter, adopted daughter and three grandchildren, even her long suffering husband. She simply could not accept the love extended her way. And by my late twenties I began to realize what a truly tormented soul she was; how much self-loathing she possessed, causing her to push away any shred of love. She could only accept love if it tormented her, or if she could torment the one extending love her way.

The final blow came the first week of February of our second winter as tenants. There was a note tacked to our door when my husband and I arrived home in the cold and dark after our hour long commute. "*My doctor has advised me that for health reasons I must request you to leave this house. You have until February 17th to vacate the premises or be evicted by court order.*" – June Gale Holloway

I marched inside to confront her with her unreasonable request. When I tried the door leading to her ell of the house, it had been nailed shut. I knew I would never cross that threshold again. My husband and I had been given just twelve days to move ourselves and the horses, mid-winter. The horse trailer was buried beneath several feet of snow. We'd have to find a place, pack, move, and find a barn to board two horses, which we could hardly afford. We'd use our vacation time to do it. I didn't care. I didn't care what it cost. I would not be subject to any more of "Mother's" conniving plans. We would be out within twelve days, and never return.

We did make the move. My marriage, already on the rocks, was now over in my mind and heart. But during this same time, my husband's mother had been diagnosed with terminal cancer, and I didn't have the heart to leave him (or her) in the midst of that ordeal. Shortly after her passing, I moved into my own apartment. Thirty days later, my husband filed for divorce. At age thirty, I was finally free to begin the long, long road of healing and recovery.

Chapter 14

Sailing Into Unchartered Waters

By now, the hole in my soul was so huge I feared I'd fall in and never climb back out. I'd spent a lifetime needing to please others to survive and to accept the conditional love offered in return. I'd learned to deny and disown my own inner guidance and intuition which seldom matched the expectations of those who held power over me in my life. My self-esteem, which had been damaged in early childhood, had been further eroded through constant emotional and psychological manipulation during my years with June.

Snow's mostly silent witness and willing participation only deepened my distrust of men. And from time to time, he too had thrown cruel words in my face over some small transgression. "You've been livin' off the fat of the land since we pulled you up outa the gutta to live with us at Holloway Farm. Yes sirree, you've been livin' off the fat of the land. And whatda we get in return? A lazy kid and a lotta guff. What you need is a little visit out behind the barn to straighten you out!" Meaning I needed a good "whippin", like Snow had endured at the hands of his Uncle Howard. The thought of a beating only struck terror and loathing in my heart.

My first husband's constant belittlement fell right in line with the treatment I'd grown accustomed to on the home front. Without realizing it, my life experience had fostered the belief that love equaled pain. I also now held a deeply imbedded subconscious belief that I was unlovable. My own parents and step-parents had rejected me. What more proof did I need?! And so like a moth to the flame, I was instinctively drawn to or would attract exactly the people who would best continue to reinforce those beliefs.

Little did I know at the time, that much deeper soul wounds and subconscious beliefs were at the core of my suffering. Years later, through shamanic practices, these wounds would eventually emerge into my awareness as part of my journey to reclaim my authentic self. My healing would require a process of unraveling from the bondage of all the experiences in my life that had reinforced my deeply held beliefs that I was unworthy, unlovable and deserving of punishment. My soul would eventually reveal those lifetimes where these deeply held wounds and beliefs had originated, and help me heal to the core of my being. But for many years, the unconscious wounds imprinted in my energy-body-soul, attracted to me exactly the experiences I did NOT want.

At work, I'd been shamed by abusive bosses who made sexual advances despite my protests, or had held me hostage through abusive work environments and humiliations both in private and public venues, further triggering my now deeply imbedded wounds. In fact, it was the work place where I now felt most powerless in the face of abuse. I began to experience post-traumatic stress symptoms, from chronic anxiety, to complete freeze and shut down of ability to think or function. It would be years before I recognized the pattern, even as I managed to be an "over achiever" and work in ever more demanding and high profile jobs.

I would find that the earliest childhood traumas, but especially the sexual abuse, would be the hardest to access and heal, and would have in many ways the most far reaching impact on my life. The shadow of sexual trauma would haunt me in many strange and bizarre ways, as my soul kept creating opportunities for me to heal and reclaim my power. "Victim", trauma energy is like a beacon, sending out a signal that attracts those who are inclined toward abusive behaviors. Both are flip sides of the same coin of trauma and loss of personal power.

When I'd find myself in the shockingly unexpected circumstance of being approached with unwanted sexual advances by friends or total strangers, my response was to freeze and shut down. It is only through the grace of some other protective force in my life, that I avoided more outright sexual trauma. For in that space of "fright" and "freeze", I could not think or act in my own defense. Fortunately for me, these would-be perpetrators did not follow through on with their unwelcomed advances.

Nevertheless, I was desperate for love and connection. But I had no healthy road map to follow. I'd give my power away early on, and lived in anxious fear of being rejected, which I was repeatedly. Until I had sufficiently healed my core wounds, I was repeatedly drawn into "relationships" where men only wanted the same kind of "user" sex I'd been forced to participate in as a child; and these men had one other trait - they each would suddenly disappear out of my life without a trace, repeating the original abandonment wound of my father. For the entire decade in my thirties, I had not a single "serious" dating relationship. No men of quality or integrity seemed to take the slightest interest in me, and with each rejection by those I did allow in, came the deepening of my shame, despair, and self-loathing.

All my friends and co-workers had siblings and family. Nearly everyone in my life was in a committed relationship, and most were raising families. Friday nights leaving work to head home for the weekend, I would feel the deep internal wound of separation and "not belonging" searing in my wounded soul. I felt more and more like a freak, and knew that my history had marked me as "damaged goods"; not in my outward appearance, or accomplishments in the world, but in the more subtle and powerful energy body and soul. I was surrounded by a "force field" that simply would not allow in what I so deeply longed for. How would I ever recover from such deeply imbedded patterns which I felt so completely powerless to change?

Food had become my one reliable comfort, my addiction, and my torment. I "needed" to have certain foods on hand to manage my anxiety and depression. Sweets were my preferred choice, and by now I'd been a secret binge eater for years. The extra pounds and yoyo dieting only added to my self-loathing, humiliation and lack of self-worth.

My low self-esteem made me an easy target to be victimized whenever even a scrap of love or affection came my way. I was a wounded soul looking to fill that hole inside so the pain would go away. Overeating, shopping sprees, or seeking love from men who were inevitably unavailable and abandoning, were how I sought to fill the gaping hole within. But these remedies only caused further wounding, perpetuating a continued downward spiral.

Age thirty was the turning point, when for the first time I sought help for the pain and anguish I was suffering. By then, I'd read many books on healing from trauma, codependence, addictions, toxic relationships, and understood my situation and issues pretty well; but understanding them intellectually was not at all the same as healing them. At first I sought out a counselor to talk with about my issues. I had just broken up with another two timing, alcoholic boyfriend.

My first question to my counselor was "Why is my self-esteem so low that I accept this kind of relationship in my life?"

The answer should have been obvious. But it wasn't until she asked how I'd been "mothered" that I really connected the two, and the tears began to flow.

Not long after, I was blessed to find a therapist who did body centered psychotherapy, with a focus on codependence and healing the wounded inner child. This, for me, was where I needed to start my deeper healing journey. For nearly two years, I participated in a weekly group therapy process, releasing feelings of grief, rage, and loss that had been held in my body and energy field for years, even decades. I began the slow journey of recovery from toxic, addictive relationships and the painful process of undoing my part in creating them.

This healing time was intense, exhausting and liberating. When our therapist told us that recovery was at least a five year process, I thought she must be joking. But in truth, I've been on a healing journey ever since.

The first summer of my healing journey, I treated myself to an incredible gift. I registered for a week long retreat on Star Island, a conference center on the Isles of Shoals, ten miles off the coast of Portsmouth, New Hampshire and Kittery, Maine. A longtime family friend had attended for years, always encouraging me to come out and experience the magic of this special place. I packed my bags in anticipation, and boarded the Thomas Leighton, heading into fresh, uncharted waters.

When I arrived at the dock, my friend Diana was there to greet me with a warm Star Island hug. Soon, I was introduced to all the conference committee members, and taken under the wing of several of them. Under their tutelage, I immediately became a "shoaler", shown all the secrets and lore of the island, while diving deep into all the conference had to offer - a wonderfully gifted conference speaker and expert on whales; a fully stocked art room and encouraging art teacher; impromptu musical gatherings on the front porch; morning and evening chapel services; a talent show, art show and conference skit; choir and the incredible sunrises and sunsets! There was also tea in the parsonage; bird watching; Polar Bear dips; low tide walks; botany walks; bonfire and folk singing; star gazing through telescopes; not to mention delicious food, served family style and fabulously interesting people and conversation. All of this was cast in a multi-generational community on a tiny island ten miles out to sea. For the first time in a long time, I was once again in Heaven!

As fate would have it, the Minister of the Week was Don Rowley, the minister of the Unitarian Church where I'd experienced my first real Christmas with the Holloways some twenty years earlier! At the close of the morning chapel, I introduced myself. As my name registered, a broad smile beamed across his face and tears came to his eyes. He told me how he had often wondered if he'd made the right decision to sign papers in support of my adoption by June. As family pastor for June's daughter, he knew only too well what a rough and rocky road it could be for me. But he had decided that the opportunities June could offer would hopefully outweigh the damages, especially in light of my dire situation at the time. I assured him, that he had indeed made the "right" decision, as was demonstrated by my presence here at Star Island! It was a joyful and fortuitous reunion sealed with a tearful hug.

For me, the most magical conference activity was evening chapel. The shoalers gather in silence on the long porch at dusk. Each is handed a candle lit lantern for the procession up the winding path, to the stone chapel on the hill. A bell ringer pulls the long rope setting a rhythm for the ancient bell in the cupola, mingling with the buoy bells in the harbor, the cry of gulls, the whoosh of waves breaking on the rocky shores and the sweep of wind through sea roses and salt air.

One by one the shoalers enter the chapel, hanging their lanterns on the wrought iron hooks and find a seat on the narrow wooden pews. Evening candlelight services are led by members of the conference, and the week's offerings were rich in wisdom, wit and tenderness. The most touching moment for me that year, and for many to come, was the singing of a song that embodied my soul's longings, and those of so many others, *Spirit of Life* by Carolyn McDade. The moving words and melody touched deeply into my heart, bringing with them healing tears.

Spirit of Life

Spirit of Life
Come unto me
Sing in my heart
All the stirrings of compassion

Blow in the wind
Rise in the sea
Move in the hand
Giving life the shape of justice

Roots hold me close
Wings set me free
Spirit of life
Come to me
Come to me

Repeating the song softly, I watch my fellow shoalers gather themselves up slowly to leave the chapel, taking more and more of the light with them. Finally I rise, taking my lantern and join the silent procession down the rocky path, weaving my way under the stars and moon, through the stinging wind and salt air, having touched the edges of something unnamable and reawakened within.

I had been welcomed into the very heart of the conference. I'd been deeply nourished, and had participated in all the creative offerings - writing, art, music, talent show, and evening chapel service. It had been cold and rainy much of the week, but I hardly noticed. I'd been warmed at the center of a group hug, and over hot cups of tea by the cozy parsonage fire and by the warm welcome. I had laughed more than I had in many years and made wonderful new shoaler friends.

When we disembarked on the Thomas Leighton for the return trip to Portsmouth, the Pelicans (the island's college aged staff), and remaining conferees began to chant, "You will come back! You will come back! You will come back!"

I cried much of the way back to the mainland, tears of gratitude, and tears of sorrow for parting again so soon. I knew I needed to bring the creative treasures I'd reclaimed on Star Island into my everyday life. And I longed for the kind of welcoming and healing community that existed there. The entire experience in many ways had been like stepping outside of time into another dimension where, for a time, my heart and soul found peace and joy.

Indeed I would "come back!" many times. Within two years, I chaired the Natural History Conference; I would serve on several committees and initiate the intergenerational women's and men's circle tradition that lasted for many seasons. I had the great blessing to lead and co-lead numerous evening candlelight services and help shape intergenerational chapel services with the island youth. Each experience was such a joyful gift to my soul!

I returned annually for more than twenty years, until many of our conference elders were with us only in spirit. Star Island became my "spirit's home" and a touch stone year to year on my personal and spiritual journey toward wholeness.

A poem written during my first retreat on Star Island spoke to the deep yearnings whispered there:

The Beckoning

I seek the rocks, the wind and sea.
I weave through your hedges and rose thickets
Where warblers and sparrows hop shyly
Amidst you bower.
The cry of the sea and gulls beckons me
And I head for your far shore
As if responding to some ancient calling;
A ritual to worship rock, sun and sea.
A modern day Druid
I am lost to sun, moon, tides and stars.
I cling to your rocks like a barnacle.
I'm yours for eternity.

Debra G. Holloway - Star Island Natural History Conference 1984

The soul does not die. It is an eternal spark of creation. When it leaves the physical body it returns to its place of rest and renewal. This place in the spirit realms will vary depending on how one has lived and died; what lessons it has completed and which lessons it will take up in a future lifetime. My wisdom teachers say our body returns to the Earth, our wisdom to the mountains, and our soul to Spirit. The soul carries the "memory" of all our lifetimes. It seeks its own destiny of fulfillment until it follows its own star home.   *- Debra LightHeart*

Chapter 15

Final Farewells

*S*hortly following my Star Island week, I had my first experience with energy medicine. It would take my healing journey into a new and rapidly accelerated direction. I went to my first polarity therapy session with the feeling of a knife in my back from the recent painful rejection by a close friend. Almost as soon as the practitioner placed her hands at my head, I began to have an emotional release....as grief and sobs shook my body. The release was short but complete, as the practitioner set about clearing and balancing my energy centers and meridians. By the end of our session, I was deeply relaxed, filled with a deep inner peace and calm I'd not known for a long time.

This was my first experience of my body as the holder of emotional energies that could be moved or awakened through touch, but more importantly, cleared. Somatic healing recognizes how the cellular tissues hold energy, including the energy of unresolved trauma. All the times I had not expressed the emotions associated with my abuse – the fear, the grief, the rage, still existed as repressed emotional energies. Over time, these repressed toxic energies, create spiritual, emotional and physical imbalances which can lead to illness and disease.

I knew this from my informal studies of energy medicine through reading, and from patterns I'd witnessed in my own biological family. The history of sexual abuse had run through generations in my family. My grandmother, mother and aunt had each had uterine cancer and hysterectomies at age forty-two. I was determined to heal myself and not repeat this legacy of disease. I continued to seek out "alternative" healing modalities and transformational practices for self-healing.

By now I had "followed my bliss", leaving a national non-profit based in Boston, and moving to Maine. I was serving as the Executive Director of a small non-profit dedicated to self-healing. It had been ten years since I'd had any contact with June or Snow. One day as I sat in my office, out of the blue, I saw a "neon blinking light" in my inner vision, flashing Snow's name. This continued numerous times a day for several days. Then, when I walked into the local grocery store to pick up a few items, inside the front door was a ten foot tall pyramid display of *Snow's Clam Chowder*! I knew Spirit was trying to get my attention, and it had something to do with Snowie.

I was sure June wouldn't take my phone call, so I finally called her cousin Malcolm, Jane's father, in New Hampshire. He verified my growing concern. Snowie was hospitalized, in stable condition, awaiting possible surgery. I knew I needed to see him. I called the hospital to get further details, and to alert them that I was on my way for a visit. With a member of my therapy group to give me moral courage, we drove several hours to the hospital. My biggest dread was having to deal with June and her causing a scene, perhaps refusing to let me see Snow. But to my surprise, she wasn't there.

When I walked in, it was a shock. Snow was sitting on the edge of his bed, looking frail and weak. He was wearing his thick post cataract surgery glasses and was unshaven; tufts of his pure white hair were standing on end. His overall appearance was that of a wise old owl. When he looked up, and our eyes met, he lit up like a Christmas tree. His nurse leaned over and yelled in his ear, "Do you know who that is, Mr. Holloway?"

"That's my daughter, Debra!" he exclaimed proudly, without skipping a beat.

The tears flowed, as I gave him a gentle hug. Although never a large man, he was now so frail. He was weak, and lay back down on the bed, head propped up on pillows as we chatted. He drifted in and out of different times and places, and I knew he was starting to lose contact with this dimension and preparing to make his transition. I had brought a CD player with a recording of ocean sounds, and asked the nurse to please bring it to the surgery, as it would help comfort him.

She assured me she would, though I wondered if it would just be tucked away out of sight.

Snow and I reminisced and caught up as best we could. It was devastating to see him here all alone, knowing June would not allow any regular contact even now. He grew tired and we finally said our goodbyes. My heart ached knowing what was coming. I left my contact information at the hospital, and drove with my friend back to Maine.

A few days later, Snow's doctor called to say Snow's condition was not good, and another surgery was not recommended. If we did nothing, he would no doubt pass away in a few days. The only other option was for Snow to be put on life support. We agreed that it would be best to let Snow, now in his mid-eighties, die a natural death and not be kept alive by machines. The doctor informed me; however, that the spouse had the final say, so June would have to agree. He offered to call and request her consent.

That afternoon, the phone rang at my desk. June was on the line.

"Hello, darling. How are you? What shall we do about our poor Snowie? I just spoke with his doctor and he thinks we should let Snow go now. He says he's not strong enough for another operation. What do you think, Dear?"

Ten years had passed without a word, a letter, a phone call. It took me a few moments to compose myself with a reply.

"Well, I think we should do as the doctor recommends. I'm sure Snow would not want to be hooked up to life support machines, don't you agree?"

"Yes, I'm sure you're right, Debra. That would be cruel, wouldn't it? After all Snowie has done for us all these years. I best call the doctor and inform him of our decision."

"Okay. Thank you for calling."

"Of course, darling, I wouldn't dream of leaving you out of such an important decision."

It was so surreal, and so June; the consummate actress.

When the doctor called me the next morning, I thought it was to tell me Snow had died. Instead, he said, "I'm sorry to tell you this, but Mrs. Holloway has requested to have Mr. Holloway put on life support."

"But we spoke on the phone yesterday!" I protested. She agreed it would be for the best! And Snow would never have wanted to be put on machines!"

I could tell the doctor sympathized, but he could not legally go against her wishes. He told me the ventilator was keeping Snow breathing now, and without it he would die.

"How long will Snow live like that?" I asked, my voice quavering with anger and grief.

"It's hard to say, but probably not more than a few weeks at most, if that. I'm so very sorry."

I thanked him for his call and hung up the phone.

I was wracked with grief, anger, despair, and feeling so helpless. I was sure June would be staying with Snow in his final days and hours, so I did not make another visit, as this would be their chance to say good-bye. A face to face meeting with her now would do neither of us any good. I later learned she never visited Snow the entire time he was in the hospital. She could not face losing him, so he would die alone.

I was in my office at work when I felt the presence of Snow's spirit. It breezed past me in a flash. I felt the rush of energy, and knew in my heart in that instant, he was on his way to the Light. I checked my messages when I got home. No call from the hospital. It would be two more days before the doctor called to tell me Snow had died and they had removed him from life support. I told the doctor I'd been expecting his call as Snow's spirit had departed two days earlier. There was silence on the other end of the line, then the doctor expressed his condolences and we hung up the phone.

On a sunny October afternoon a few days later while I was at work, I heard footsteps coming down the hall. When I looked up, the office assistant was carrying a small square box wrapped in brown paper, her eyes glistening with tears. I was sobbing by the time she crossed the room, gently placing the box containing Snow's ashes on my desk. She put her arms around me as I rocked in profound grief for this dear man who had so touched my life, and the terrible waste of the ten long years we'd missed sharing at the end of his life.

My grief rolled between storms of intense pain, and surprising waves of joy. I took a few of Snow's ashes to my favorite place on an island off Portland, scattering them among the huge Oak trees, and on the bluffs overlooking the sea. I stayed well past sunset, and walked the mile back around the island back to my car cloaked in darkness.

Part of Snow I'd keep close to me. The rest I would take to Boothbay. And on an appointed blustery, sparkling fall day, a friend accompanied me to Snowie's boyhood town. After touring the Boothbay Harbor, I crossed the footbridge in memory of Snow one more time, dropping some coins in the water as he and his sister had done many decades before. Then my friend and I drove to a secluded cove, and I scattered Snow's ashes on the rolling seas, his home once more.

Three weeks before Christmas the following year, I was enrolled in an empowerment weekend workshop intensive led by gifted creators of a new paradigm and teaching model for helping people vision and step into the lives they truly want. Their book had captured my imagination, and I knew I needed a large dose of self-empowerment to move forward in my life. The three day workshop was challenging, highly experiential, and transformational. As it turned out, it also came at a crucial time in my journey.

That weekend I was having the oddest experience. When I looked in the mirror, I did not recognize myself. What I saw, was an old hag. I couldn't see my facial features, as they'd been just prior to the start of the workshop. There was also this cloak of heavy energy around me, weighing me down. I felt listless, and wondered how I'd make it through the grueling twelve hour day schedule.

Mid-way through the weekend we reached a crucible moment in my process, and the question was put to me by one of the facilitators, "Do you want to live?"

I sat in numbed silence.

"Until you commit to live, you will not be empowered in your life. Debra, do you want to live?"

My mind sped through a life review, all that had been loved and lost, my recent move to Maine, the heaviness I was now feeling, what had inspired me to attend the workshop.

Did I want to live? Did I want to die? No, I wanted to live. But I wanted to live a different life than I had lived up to now.

"Yes, I want to live!" I finally declared, though I felt like my very life force was being sucked out of me, and it was.

The following week as I processed and integrated from the Empowerment weekend, I still didn't feel like myself. Finally, I sat down with one of our staff facilitators at work, who was also a gifted psychic, and asked her to tune in to my energy field. She immediately picked up on the "heavy" presence, and said, "Someone close to you is dying, and trying to take you with them."

I knew in a flash, it must be June. I had just written her a Christmas card a few days earlier. It was on my desk, waiting until I called her daughter, Essjay, for June's mailing address. It would have been my first effort at contact in ten years. But I never had the chance to mail the card.

Two days later, Essjay called to say June had died. She had refused all food, water and medications in recent days, and had instructed her caregivers and staff NOT to contact any family members. I thought the fact that staff did not contact family, despite June's wishes, was highly irregular. But I think all of us simply felt a sense of relief for her emotional suffering to be over. She had pushed everyone in her family away permanently, and died alone. June was an atheist, and did not believe in any Spiritual presence, or after life of the soul. I had known for years that she was terrified of death. December was also the time of year she sank into her deepest depression over a jilted love during her adult years, from which she had never recovered. I prayed that when her time finally came, she had found some peace.

For those of us left behind, June wasn't quite finished. Against June's wishes, her daughter Essjay and I agreed we should have a memorial service for our mother in Massachusetts. She set about contacting many members of extended family, most of whom I'd never met. Since it was ten days before Christmas, I brought presents for Essjay and her children whom I'd grown up with as "cousins". We'd all enjoyed each other's company on the limited basis June permitted, and now as adults we often shared holidays or vacation time together. I drove down with a dear friend from Maine who offered to accompany me for moral support.

I parked in front of the church, hurrying inside to help with the final preparations. The truth was we all wanted to put this behind us before the holidays and the New Year. With all the years of silence between us, and all the issues left unresolved between my "Mother" and me, I hadn't found any words coming from my heart to share on short notice for the service. Nor did I ever shed a single tear of grief for June's passing. What I did grieve, were all the wasted years and what might have been. For the service, all I could muster was the reading of a short poem, with no personal commentary whatsoever. I left that to others.

When it was time for the reception, I went to get the presents from the car so I wouldn't forget to give them out as people were leaving. I was anxious to meet some of the interesting people and family members I'd heard June talk about over the years. But when I stepped outside, my car was gone! Then I saw it parked across the street at a garage. I walked over to inquire. A large sign was hanging over the door: *This Garage Guarded by a Pit Bull with AIDS.*

"This is just great," I thought out loud. "Just great!"

The owner was as grim as his sign.

"Yah cah was pahked illegally. So the cops called me to tow it".

"How much do I owe you for towing?"

"Fifty bucks."

"Fifty bucks, to haul it fifty feet", I fumed to myself.

I wanted to pay the towing charge and get out of there as fast as I could. I turned to go fetch my wallet.

"Well, yah cah won't be goin' nowheas. The registration has expired, and yah cahn't drive an unregistered cah in Massachusetts. Guess yah stuck right heah."

By now, the guests at the memorial service were enjoying the reception food, and gathered in small groups catching up or reminiscing about happier times. I was looking for a phone, phone book and calling the police department for assistance. The officer on the phone confirmed that my car had been impounded for expired registration. I pleaded my case, and he agreed to send a police officer to meet with me. Then I alerted Essjay and her three grown children to what had transpired. There was a pause, then in unison we all crowed, "It's June! She didn't want this party, and now's she's having the last laugh!"

But it wasn't funny to me or my friend. She had to get back to Maine to pick up her children at the babysitter, and I had animals to care for at home. I couldn't spend several days in Massachusetts waiting to get a new registration from Maine! My stomach was in knots. By now guests were leaving, and most had little interest in meeting me at this point anyway. I anxiously awaited the arrival of the police officer. When he walked through the door, I patted myself on each shoulder, requesting an EXTRA LARGE SIZE pair of angel wings and angel teams to be here, right now to please help me! We simply had to get back to Maine by early evening.

I met with the officer and told him my plight. He surveyed the memorial table where we'd laid out some of June's personal mementos – her framed Charter Member Certificate from the National Association of Social Workers, a copy of her published book, a rare enlarged photo of her with Snow and her signature sneakers…this pair was gold.

I supposed because it was a memorial service, and the fact that my registration had just expired in the midst of my step-mother's death, the officer took pity on me. Or perhaps divine intervention played a helping hand. In any event, he wrote up a permit for me to drive the car to Maine, where I was to register it within three days or face a heavy fine. I thanked him for being our "Christmas Angel", and we all sighed a great sigh of relief.

I retrieved my car, parked in the lot behind the church and at last distributed the bags of Christmas gifts to Essjay and her adult children. Then there was one more thing. By now we were all on the verge of hysterics, from the bizarre turn of the day. Essjay disappeared for a minute or two, and returned carrying a small metal box. It was June's ashes. Oh, No! The box made its way around the circle two times. Each time being quickly passed from one family member to the next. Eventually, the box of ashes stopped with me. June wished to join Snowie in having her ashes cast into the waters off Boothbay Harbor. I brought her ashes back to Maine with me. The following spring, Essjay and I would journey to Boothbay to grant June her final wish.

Laughter was our relief that day, for each of us bore deep scars from June's behaviors over the years, which had left a trail of broken promises and cruel actions that cut deeply. Yet I also felt bitter sadness for the extraordinary woman that June had been in so many ways. She'd had a keen intellect and insatiable hunger for knowledge; she'd been a poet, prolific writer and self-published author; a talented seamstress and amateur architect; a debutante, designer, historian, teacher, camp counselor, social worker, non-profit executive, wife, mother, step-mother and grandmother. She created extraordinary homes, threw fabulous parties, liked to drive fast cars, and had her own heart broken too many times.

And somewhere, in her past, there had been trauma, and cruelty, creating deeply imbedded fears. One is not born cruel and afraid; one does not suffer from panic attacks and deep depression without cause. Perhaps the biggest sorrow I feel after all these years, is not really knowing all of June's story, and what caused her to have so much self-loathing, that she cut herself off from those who loved her; and the fact that although she sought the help of psychiatrists and doctors, she never found the path that would help her heal her emotional pain and soul wounds.

The majority of June's precious heirlooms she'd donated to museums or given to wealthy family members in her later years, to continue being passed down to future generations. Most of her financial resources had been used to pay for her assisted living care. What was left, she willed to her niece. June's own daughter, adopted daughter and three grandchildren were not mentioned in her estate planning. It came as no surprise to any of us. It was final verification of her closed and broken heart.

But June didn't quite get her final wishes. Her niece contacted the attorney, and insisted that the remaining sum be divided equally between her two daughters. This was a very kind and generous gesture, which put a bit of salve on old wounds. Essjay and I divided the few remaining items, some set aside for her grown children. There was no angst, or greed. None of us could carry on the legacy that June had grown up with, a life of wealth and privilege; and a life that had also come at a very high price for June and those she loved.

I was very grateful for the sum which was enough for a down payment on my dream home – "a little cape, with a little barn, on a little land". When I purchased the property on Joy Valley Road, I knew I had finally "come home".

Chapter 16

True Love Comes Calling

$\mathcal{A}$fter a year of receiving the benefits of energy medicine, I was also beginning to hear my calling as a healer, even, as like many before me, I was still walking the path of "the wounded healer". I was working full-time in a rewarding but demanding job as a development, programs and public relations director. Nevertheless, I enrolled in a 650 hour weekend professional training in Polarity Therapy.

Polarity draws its name from the measureable electric currents of energy that course through the body. These currents have a positive and negative pole, thus creating the flow of energy throughout the meridians and other energy centers of the body. Disruption of the natural flow of these energies contributes to ill health and disease. Polarity is the synthesis of holistic health practiced by Dr. Randolph Stone, who studied numerous energy medicine modalities which he integrated into his medical practice. He had studied India's 3,000 year old Ayurvedic medicine and integrated aspects of this holistic healing model into his work with patients, including protocols for nutrition, internal cleansing, body postures and yoga, as well as energy balancing as pathways to health and vitality.

Dr. Stone authored seven volumes on polarity energy medicine, and his pioneering work continued on through the students he taught and mentored. He played an integral role in bringing holistic practices back into the fold as an integral element missing in modern medicine. The school in which I enrolled expanded on the teachings of Dr. Stone with practices one would need to experience to believe.

I would learn the true power of high vibrational healing in my first class. It was my turn to receive the work we had just learned. When the fellow student, placed his hand on my hip, I immediately launched into a huge emotional release, crying and wailing, lost in my pain and emotion. I had no memories associated with the feelings that were clearly still held in my physical body. The instructors came and stood by me for a few minutes as I lay venting emotions. Then I heard one say, "This has probably gone on long enough. Why don't we just clear it?" She held a large quartz crystal, sweeping it through my energy field, while directing amplified healing energy to me through the crystal. In a few moments, my emotional release was over, the trauma energy had been cleared. The instructor asked the student to continue with the polarity energy balancing practice we were learning.

That one experience set me on a new course of healing in my life, for now I knew I did not need to re-process every event, every wound. While there had been great value in the previous therapies I'd experienced, I knew this course of healing was moving me forward in a new way. My polarity studies included considerable esoteric work in addition to the body work portions of the training. I was introduced to the energy field, clearing chakras and the aura and other subtle energies. I learned how to magnify healing with quartz crystals, which deeply resonate with our body's own crystalline structures and like us, have a negative and positive charge, or energy current. We learned how to work the therapeutic use of color, and I learned how to move and clear energy with sound. All of this more subtle energy work was grounded in extensive study of anatomy, massage and body work practice, nutrition, internal cleanses and polarity yoga.

Essential to our practice was working in sacred space, calling in each individual's highest healing teams and divine guidance. We learned how to tune into and trust our own inner healer and inner guidance to be of highest and most aligned assistance to our clients. This was rich and deep work, which moved me forward light years in my personal healing, while opening channels to ancient healing ways which had simply been waiting to be reawakened.

My personal life moved forward and expanded in new ways as well. I set up my healing practice in my new home, and to make it official, I scheduled a meeting with the town's Code Enforcement

Officer. I set the stage as best I could, wondering how I'd explain the kind of "home business" I was starting. I was pretty sure Polarity Therapy was not a household word in this small town. The meeting proved most interesting and engaging. This man was unlike any other town or city official I'd met, and we touched on several areas of common ground in the course of our conversation. Then we began to "see each other" across the room at the local community arts center and chat during intermissions. It would take several months, but eventually, Fred asked me out on a date.

About two years prior, I'd gone to see a gifted psychic who channeled a group of beings. Naturally, I wanted to know about any possibilities in my future for a relationship. She or "they" assured me one was coming, "One who will cherish you as you longed to be cherished." After a pause they added, "You will know him by his collar". My friends and I had pondered the meaning of those words for some time. I prayed that it wouldn't be another unavailable man, this time in the form of a priest or punk rocker!

One evening, I was working in the garden, all hot and sweaty. A song had come on the radio that always brought tears, Mary Chapin Carpenter's rendition of John Lennon's song, *Grow Old Along With Me*. How I ached for a love to grow old with and I wiped the tears away with my soil blackened hand. Just then I noticed Fred walking up the road and coming my way.

"Oh, damn!" I thought. "I look like Hell!" That did nothing to diminish his smile or his invitation to join him for a cruise on the Songo River Queen on Lake Sebago, that Saturday.

"It's a fund raiser for the fire department. I bought the tickets quite a while back, and at the time I didn't know why I bought two. I know it's short notice, so if you can't make it I understand." He looked nervously at the ground as if waiting for the rejection that was sure to follow.

"I'd love to go!" I replied, hoping I didn't sound too eager, but genuine. A smile lit up his face and we set our plans in motion.

Fred arrived in his pickup truck at the appointed time that Saturday. He'd brought us a picnic lunch to share on the boat. He opened my door, like a true gentleman, and as I sat watching him climb in on the driver's side, I saw it. There, on the steering column of his truck, was a well-worn, red dog collar, with the dog tags still dangling from it. I felt a chill course through my body. "You will know him by his collar." When I inquired, he said the collar was from a beloved dog who had been his constant companion during his years as a land surveyor. He simply kept this with him as a token of their deep bond and connection.

And so, a sweet, loving and nourishing two year courtship and relationship unfolded, surpassing anything I thought possible for me. Fred was kind and thoughtful and we shared a love of nature and the outdoors, animals, music, and the same impassioned political bearings.

Here was a hard-working man with a kind heart, who had his own crosses in life to bear, but who rose above his own pain to be of service to others.

Within a year, we decided I'd sell my home on Joy Valley Road, to purchase a home together, one that abutted a thousand acre game preserve and conservation area. The following year we hosted a backyard September wedding at our new home, surrounded by family and friends. Together, we had crossed a threshold into a chapter of utter joy and contentment. At last, I'd found my soul mate, and was sharing a life partnership based in love, respect and a mutual love of nature and the out of doors. It was the most joyous time of my adult life.

Fred and I relished our outdoor adventures, exploring waterways by kayak, woods and mountains on foot. Our doggie companions added joy to our lives, along with our two cats, a rescued rabbit and a baby chipmunk saved from the jaws of the neighbor's lawnmower. We explored the game preserve behind our house on a regular basis, discovering a wide diversity of flora and fauna, and many species unknown to us in this unique Pitch Pine Barrens.

In summer, we foraged for quarts of wild blueberries, along with the deer and coyotes that ate their share. At night we slept out on our summer porch, serenaded by Whip-poor-wills, as we were bathed by the light of the stars and the ever-changing moon. In the morning, we'd awaken to hummingbirds at the feeders and morning song birds. In winter, we took to cross country skiing, and ice skating. With access to frozen wetlands and bogs we delighted in exploring new territory, now easily traversed on skis, across the dazzling snow covered landscape.

We soon learned "The Outback" as we called it, was also a magnet for loud beer parties, the burning of stolen cars and dumping of trash. ATV's were being ridden through the fragile wetlands and loud motor cross racing went unchecked. An unofficial shooting range was active at all hours, including Sunday mornings. We even were witness to the poaching of deer and illegal duck hunting. It seemed the game preserve was home to "wild life", but not always the kind we'd been anticipating. Though we had sought sanctuary miles away from the nearest city or town, the peacefulness was shattered on a regular basis, in ways I found very emotionally distressing. I felt more and more violated by the numerous activities on the unmonitored game preserve that defiled the landscape, while stressing and even killing resident wildlife and destroying fragile habitat.

Soon, Fred and I set about cleaning up the landscape, as we became a regular "presence" on the preserve. We often doused smoldering fires left from parties, and on occasion, even had to call the fire department. Fred personally removed tons of trash over the months; I conducted ceremonies working with the nature and guardian spirits to help shift the destructive and abusive energies that had become the norm. During this time, we experienced numerous magical encounters in the Outback, some so profound, I was certain they were offered to us as gifts of gratitude from the spirits of the land herself.

As the months passed, the energies shifted. The parties and fires occurred less frequently and then ceased all together; the ATV's stayed on the marked trails, and the motor cross riders found a more suitable raceway nearby. The Nature Conservancy took an interest in the barrens and began to conduct prescribed burns to help manage and maintain this unique ecosystem which requires fire to thrive.

We had been stewards of the land and had worked cooperatively with the nature spirits to help restore balance, as well as the peace and quiet. But those that benefitted most, were the numerous birds and wildlife that called this place home at least some of the year: nesting Red Winged Black Birds, Whip-Poor-Wills, Nighthawks, Great Blue Herons, various hawks and many varieties of warblers and other songbirds; the beaver returned after our "clearing" of the land, along with moose. Also in residence were deer, red fox, coyotes, turtles, muskrats, chipmunks and porcupines. In spring and fall, the wetlands were resting places for migrating birds including Canadian Geese, Blue Teal and Hooded Merganser Ducks. The Outback was at first glance, a "barren" place. But in fact, this was an ecosystem rich in diversity and beauty; a place generous with gifts, for those who took the time to really see and know her.

Chapter 17

Unhealed Wounds and Patterns

I remained deeply committed to continue my personal healing, and to follow my soul's calling as a healer. Energy medicine had opened a gateway, promoting deep healing and transformation that I could never have accessed through talk therapy. Energy medicine moves blocked energy and can clear the "triggers" that activate the nervous system's fight or flight response. Energy medicine also serves to calm our "reptilian brain" and our limbic system and activates our parasympathetic system and "God Brain". While the former keeps us trapped in the patterns of triggering old wounds, the latter allows us to experience ourselves as multi-dimensional spiritual beings. From an expanded, relaxed state, our mind, body and soul come into alignment, and true peace, joy and healing are accessible. With practice, we begin to remember this, our natural state of being.

I desperately wanted to make the transition from non-profit work to my calling as a healer. Yet, paralyzing fear came up around financial stability, and giving up the livelihood that had been my chosen career for nearly twenty years. But every year the expectations of my job grew, and I was frequently at the brink of exhaustion. After six years, I was approaching burn out, and was experiencing post-traumatic stress symptoms under the growing pressures at work. Then one night, I had a dream that helped give me the impetus I needed to let go.

I was standing in a horse show arena. A beautiful show jumper mare was being ridden over the jump course. She made her way gracefully around the course with a clean round. As the audience applauded, the fences were raised and her male rider took her again over the round of fences. Though she struggled over the last two fences, she again jumped a clean round. Once more, the fences were raised. The mare was tiring now, but cleared the first few fences cleanly. But when she came to the giant triple bar spread, she slipped on takeoff, crashed into the obstacle and fell, landing on her side. Her rider landed clear and ran to her side, but she didn't move. Men in orange vests came into the stadium, grabbed the exhausted and injured mare by her tail and dragged her out of the arena to the booing of the crowd.

I knew I was that mare in my dream; the arena was my workplace, and the male rider, my boss, with ever higher and higher expectations.

I also knew if I couldn't do the job anymore, they'd simply find someone who could, at least for a while. I did not want to wait until I collapsed at work or worse. I knew my soul was crying out, and I needed to listen. Shortly after that dream, I did make the courageous leap into my new life as a healing arts practitioner.

Reclaiming my soul would require much deeper work before I would find the peace and the empowerment I was seeking. But for a time I thrived in the energy of Polarity Therapy. For two years, I worked from home offering sessions and women's circles. My clients healed long time issues, moved through difficult life transitions more easily and found relief from a multitude of emotional and physical issues. Like me, they enjoyed the feeling of deep peace and tranquility that accompanied sessions, and the sense of being deeply nourished on the soul level.

But I knew I had more to heal, and a great deal more to learn about healing. I had cleared many layers, but I sensed there were much deeper, denser layers, yet to be addressed. And they were still running aspects of my life in ways I could not fathom. I still had not cleared and healed the repeating patterns of suffering in my life, usually relating to my deepest issues. I knew a core wound for me was abandonment. It was a theme that had played out in every relationship leading up to my most recent second marriage. I traced the origin to the fact I never knew my father. I always felt that his abandonment had been a big contributor to my "hole in the soul", in addition to my mother, who was unequipped at age seventeen to raise a child. In time, I would discover a much older and deeper origin to my abandonment wounds.

As I continued with my polarity therapy practice, I noticed there were clients who despite feeling great after sessions, retained core wounding patterns. And although I received regular sessions myself, certain patterns, and an emotional angst would return between sessions, or with certain triggers. Then one day, I happened upon a copy of Sandra Ingerman's book *Soul Retrieval*, and everything in it resonated within me.

Soon I was seeking out an introductory class in shamanic journeying and did the classic journey weekend training with gifted teachers in Port Clyde, Maine who were graduates of The Foundation for Shamanic Studies, founded by Michael Harner, Ph.D. The Foundation is credited with introducing core shamanism to "non-indigenous" peoples on a global scale. Michael Harner's work set in motion a global resurgence in the study and practice of shamanism. Soon, other teachers would join the ranks in bringing powerful, ancient shamanic healing practices out of the shadows of fear and misunderstanding, restoring them their rightful place of service to humanity and the Earth.

My first shamanic weekend opened up new dimensions of awareness and healing for me. I also knew on a deep level, that if I chose the shamanic path, it would change my life dramatically, in directions I was not currently ready or willing to travel. But the seeds had been planted. I followed up with a weekend shamanic retreat learning how to work with the spirits of nature, and again, my soul felt deep resonance with the work. The shamanic retreats were activating something deep and familiar within my being; something I'd been touching the edges of since childhood.

When we take steps in the direction of our soul's calling, there is often a backlash. Most often it is our resistance to change, and subconscious fears often planted deeply with good reason. But sometimes it takes perspective to fully understand what our soul is trying to show us, how it is guiding us, and at times setting us on an entirely new path.

Not long after my introduction to shamanic healing, something in my soul was birthing and it was painful. My abandonment issues were up. I was no longer feeling the deep connection with my husband, and I could not seem to find an entry point from which we could communicate what was going on for us in our relationship and our marriage. The wall of silence and withdrawal was triggering my old abandonment wounds and a "survival response" ingrained since early childhood. Moving had been the response to drama after drama. Crisis had been in the air with every move. Without realizing it at the time, I stepped into this familiar pattern in order to distract myself from my painful inner turmoil and feeling of helplessness in healing my marriage. I thought moving closer to "community" and our jobs would be the outer solution to my inner crisis.

So, I persuaded my husband we should buy a darling little house on the river....in a nearby town where he worked....and closer to the community I craved. He had a lot of legitimate concerns about the house which I was reluctant to see, as I was enamored with this waterfront home on the river in a charming neighborhood. I was completely blind to the pitfalls and limitations the property offered compared to our current home on over an acre, adjacent to the game preserve. At the time, the abuse of the Outback was at its peak, causing me great emotional anguish and distress, even as Fred and I were working to "clear" the land of these assaults. A move would be my escape route from this source of pain, and hopefully toward some unknown remedy for my inner turmoil.

The night after our second look at the property I'd set my heart on buying, I saw my husband gazing out the window of our home, tears silently rolling down his cheeks. I realized in an instant what a mistake I was making in steering our lives and our marriage in this direction. Though we had put $1,000 earnest money down, it seemed we should re-think and reconsider our plans. I did not want a move if that would cost us our long term happiness, or worse, our marriage. It seemed to me, $1,000 would be a small price to pay to avert disaster. I asked Fred several times to talk with me about it. He simply couldn't consider not going through with the agreement, and wouldn't discuss a change of direction for our lives, which I now feared was heading for a steep cliff.

We were scheduled to meet with the real estate agent, and my heart was heavy as the hour approached. As the realtor presented the agreement to me for co-signature, I considered tearing it up and forfeiting our deposit. But I ignored my inner compass. Fate seemed to be at hand. I could not summon the courage to tear up the contract.

Before my signature dried on the page, there was a terrible thud, as a huge hawk flew into the garage window. Stunned, we all turned to see what had happened. The hawk lay on his back, and I feared it had broken its neck. But it began to move and soon stood on wobbly legs, then flew to a nearby branch shaking its head, and getting its bearings before it flew low across the thicket. I knew in my heart, and by the wrenching tug in my stomach, we had just sealed our fate on a future very different from the one we'd envisioned not so very long ago. Hawk had brought a message that day, and I shivered to think what would lie ahead, or just around the corner. I knew, like that hawk, I had flown into an illusion. The move was not an auspicious one for our marriage, as the timing of hawk's message had already confirmed, just moments too late for me to remedy by following my gut instincts.

Not being able to speak honestly about what was really going on and what each of us really wanted and needed, was the weakest link in my relationship with my husband. The more I tried to "fix" my marriage, the more it unraveled. Patterns of wounding often experienced as children, of not being able to speak our truth, or not being heard by ones we love and trust, who also have power over us, can set us up for disastrous relationships.

Without professional assistance to help heal and learn new communication practices, many couples cannot successfully navigate the inevitable challenges of sharing a life. Coupled with patterns, traumas and core beliefs held in the subconscious mind-body-soul, all systems are crying out for healing, for resolution. We instinctively attract to us those who will readily activate these wounds for the purpose of healing them. Yet, few among us have the road maps for accessing, navigating and healing this terrain within ourselves or our relationships.

Yet, sometimes an act of courageous honesty can heal old hurts and help set a soul free. My beloved cousin, Jane, would help teach me the power of such honesty, love and forgiveness, not long after my fateful move.

Chapter 18

Our Only Purpose in Life

When Jane was diagnosed with a recurring cancer, we had an unexpected reunion after several years with no contact. It would prove to be a time of healing for us both.

I was selling my art at a local arts and crafts event in Maine. A woman and I struck up a conversation, and when she was about to leave, she handed me her card. Seeing she was from Gloucester, Massachusetts I asked," By any chance do you know my cousin, Jane Winsor?"

Her eyes lit up. "Why yes, as a matter of fact, I'm attending her art opening this evening! Here's one of the invitations. It's a fund raiser to help Jane with her medical expenses.

"Her medical expenses?"

"Well, yes. Perhaps you don't know, but Jane has been diagnosed with brain cancer."

"No, I didn't know", I stammered in stunned surprise. "Will you do me a favor and bring her this print, and let me write her a note on one of my cards. Would you please take these to her tonight? I'd be so grateful."

The woman graciously agreed and departed.

A couple of days later, Jane called and we made plans for a visit. When she opened the door, my heart wept with joy. Jane's face was swollen from the chemo treatments, and on her bald head she wore a beautifully woven cap. Her spirit shone brightly through her eyes, despite the obvious rigors of her treatments. Her art sale had sold out, raising thousands of dollars toward her medical expenses.

While she fixed us a cup of tea, I surveyed her Gloucester bungalow for the first time. It was filled with the treasures of the artist, explorer, and independent, spirited woman that she'd always been. Yet, the house was heavy with stagnant energy, and I felt the presence of death was not far off. She told me some of her pets had recently died quite suddenly, and she tried to make light of mistaking the bath tub for the toilet to take a pee. But Jane had a glow about her that came from a deep inner place, and she spoke from a depth that reflected the journey of the soul she was now undertaking.

She wasted no time in raising an incident that happened decades earlier when we were teenagers. She had come for a visit and we'd spent the afternoon making art. When she left, a small watercolor painting remained on the table. It was a salt marsh scene, sweet and evocative. I leaned it up against the pile of books on the table without a thought. A few days later, when June happened into the room as I was painting with some watercolors, she picked up the little piece, admiring it.

"Did you paint this?"

I paused, admiring the sweet painting. "Yes," I replied, wishfully. Had I only known what my little lie would cost!

The truth is, when the question arose, I couldn't seem to remember where the painting had come from. I certainly wished I had painted it, but I hadn't.

"Oh, it's very nice; your best yet," June pronounced, and then went about her business.

About a month later, Jane and her parents came for a visit. I had grown to dread our tea time visitors, as June had taken to making copies of some of my writings without my knowledge, and conducted readings of my work, to my dismay and the uncomfortable embarrassment of our guests. But this day, to my relief, I didn't see any papers tucked on the corner of the table waiting to be read aloud.

June disappeared to put the kettle on for tea, and returned holding the small water color painting aloft, announcing, "Look at the lovely painting Debra did recently! Why it's nearly as good as one of Jane's!"

A hushed silence fell over the room. I must have blushed ten shades of red, and cast my eyes to the floor, wishing I could fall through a crack and disappear. I couldn't look at Jane. I felt so ashamed and was too embarrassed to say anything, to speak the truth. The truth was that Jane was a far superior artist period. She was extremely gifted. I loved her dearly, but was jealous, too, at the ease and grace of her gift, especially when compared to my own much more humble efforts.

June kept prattling on about how talented I was, and how she was considering enrolling me in art school; all the while, knowing perfectly well I hadn't painted the piece, and that all of us were simmering in a stew of embarrassment, shame, guilt, humiliation and anger.

That day had never been discussed until now. I was shocked to learn how it had haunted Jane even more darkly than I could have imagined. She told me the lesson she came away with that day was, "not to be too good"; and how her gifts as an artist became tainted by her fear of attracting the attentions born of envy, competition and betrayal. I was stunned. I told her how truly sorry I was, as we wept, hugging each other in relief and forgiveness. I knew how important this piece of healing must have been for both our souls, as I reflected on the unlikely circumstances that reunited us at this time, after so many years.

I offered Jane some healing body work, in between our childhood reminiscing and browsing through old photos of ourselves riding our horses, dressed for Halloween Trick-Or-Treating and playing on the beach together, all those years ago.

Later, Jane woke me in the middle of the night to share the heavy vanilla scent of the white climbing vine outside her bedroom window. The full moon gilded the luminous white flowers that only bloomed at night; and Jane's bald head glowed like Luna herself in the moon light. We sat in silence drinking in the nectar of the heavy fragrance and this sweet interlude which would be our last.

Then Jane spoke softly, as if from some place far away. "You know, Deb, when all is said and done, life is really simple. Our only purpose is to love one another. That's it! All we're here to do is love each other." And we held each other in a warm embrace. Then after a long pause, she continued, whispering in my ear, "Deb, there's something else I need to tell you. You're meant to be an author. You're already a wonderful writer, and someday, people are going to be reading your books! I just know it! I feel it in my bones."

Then she shivered with the evening chill, and I tucked her in snug under the covers, stroking her beautiful bald head and swollen cheeks as she quickly drifted back to sleep, hot tears streaming down my face. Her face gleamed in the moonlight in a stunningly peaceful repose. It broke my heart to know she was preparing to make her journey Home. But I was ever so grateful for her courage in allowing us to heal our past and reclaim the only thing that really mattered in any of our lives....the capacity to love and be loved.

Often, it is our very "woundedness" that sets us on our path of power and spiritual awakening. Healers often hear their call to service while they are navigating their own healing journey. Our call to "healing" is first and foremost a personal call to heal ourselves, and then to extend our healing experience and wisdom to others.

The gifts of grace offered through the shamanic realms are extraordinary. The dimensions of "non-ordinary reality" are alive with spiritual allies, teachers and healing teams ready to assist us on our healing and spiritual journey. They exist outside of time, and are not motivated by ego or power, but by compassion and love. They help us see things about ourselves that are keeping us bound to our suffering, and they offer the energetic tools and resources to set ourselves free. It is always our choice, and no true spiritual ally or teacher will act on our behalf without our request or permission.   - Debra LightHeart

Chapter 19

Path of the Wounded Spiritual Warrior

$\mathcal{L}$ife patterns sourcing from our wounds can cost us greatly, keeping us chained to the past, despite our best efforts. I wanted desperately to be free of these, and enrolled in a two year shamanic healing and training that promised to heal wounds at their source, to align me with my destiny, and to restore the sources of power I had lost so long ago.

Shamanic healing is the oldest healing modality, originating with the earliest indigenous peoples and surviving, even thriving today. The roots of shamanism run deep through the heart of humanity and live in our DNA, connecting us to the profound wisdom of the Earth, Spirit and the Cosmos. The shamanistic world view is one of unity, where creation is perceived as living energy. All is an expression of Creation, and all has power and wisdom. The Earth and all her creations are viewed as sacred, carrying wisdom and "medicine".

The shaman travels with her spirit body between the world of "ordinary reality" to the realms of "non-ordinary reality", to access wisdom from spirit helpers and healing teams. She or he brings back this wisdom not only for self-healing, but more often to help the healing of individuals, families, communities and the Earth.

The doorway to the realms of "non-ordinary reality" is accessible to nearly all those who seek to enter. The process is remarkably simple and straightforward. The shamanic journey consciousness is readily awakened by the simple, rapid beating of a drum at 200 – 250 beats per minute. This rhythm creates a light "trance" state, opening the mind to higher states of consciousness while activating the deeper wisdom of our soul. Shamanic trainings and journeying workshops have grown exponentially across the United States and Europe in recent years. Ninety-eight percent of participants are able to journey effectively almost immediately, having powerful direct experiences in the sacred realms of Spirit.

Another fundamental principle of shamanism is that the shaman is not bound by linear time, which is an artificial human construct. The shaman, shamanic practitioner, creates and works in "sacred space" which is timeless, and aligned with the forces of the universe. It is during this state of being the shaman is able to heal events of the past and access wisdom from the future. Since healing is not bound by time, wounded souls can be healed from events from many lifetimes ago and soul patterns can be cleared, so they no longer are passed on to future generations. Healing is available for those who have passed over into Spirit, just as it is for the living.

Shamans work at the energetic level where all things come into form and can therefore be transformed. They are assisted by benevolent helping spirits who have extraordinary love, compassion and wisdom. For a shaman to be a healer and not a sorcerer, the ego must be well honed toward service to others and not toward gathering of power for personal gain or to harm, control or manipulate others, even "for their own good"!

A reputable shaman does not work on behalf of another's healing without their permission; this is a form of sorcery. Even if one is in a comma, permission of the soul can be accessed. The shaman must remain very vigilant on her path, of her own light and her own shadow. Only by forming strong relationships with their spirit helpers and being open to their soul's wisdom that is not bound by ego or mind, can the shaman walk with grace, integrity and power. Only then, can he or she truly be of service to others and the world around them.

My journey around the medicine wheel would be the most deeply profound and challenging of my life, accessing core wounds I never would have uncovered on my own. The magnified healing field of group work, combined with the Peruvian medicine lineage I was stepping into, along with the caliber of the teachers and the "invisible" spiritual healing teams invited to assist us, set all participants on a course of self-discovery unlike any we'd experienced before.

We gathered at a small retreat center in Connecticut. All eighty of us were engaged in shamanic training, though we were in different classes, and levels of experience. The intensity and power of the healing work was palpable and visible as each participant's extraordinary transformation unfolded before our eyes. Equally astounding, was the diversity of participants – hospital administrators, therapists, plumbers and electricians, artists, healers, bankers, doctors and truck drivers. We had come together from five different nations, heeding our inner call to this deeply transformational path of empowerment. The Seeds of Light to awaken our human consciousness to new levels, had indeed, been scattered far and wide. And one by one, they were being activated and nurtured. But first, each of us had much to release and heal.

I arrived at my first class not knowing what to expect. Nothing could have prepared me for what my soul was about to reveal. We had just learned the first healing process for clearing the chakras of stagnant or blocked energy; and how to fill the chakras with pure essence from Spirit. In just a few minutes, the formerly clogged chakras spinning backwards were now open and spinning rapidly clockwise, once again drawing in the "sami", nourishing life force energies into the physical body.

When it was time to practice the work, we counted off by number, and my partner and I decided to work in the small chapel along with several other pairs of students. I practiced the work first. I began by opening my energy field around my partner as we'd been shown, then moved to hold deepening points at the base of her skull, monitoring her breathing. I tested her seven primary energy centers, "chakras", for blocked or dense energies and used my "khuya" healing stone to help clear the heavy energies. Once the dense energies had cleared, I illuminated her chakras with pure divine light. After our short session, all her chakras were radiant and spinning rapidly clockwise, indicating they were clear and aligned. After we exchanged our experiences of giving and receiving the work, I lay down to receive my first chakra illumination through this Peruvian medicine lineage.

I relaxed immediately into the healing energy, and felt my partner's hands gently at my head gently holding release points to promote relaxation, as she encouraged me to breathe deeply. In less than a minute, I was viewing myself in another time and place. I was experiencing my first spontaneous past life memory. It was like a dream where I was both viewing the dream and the one being viewed. At the same time, I was receiving auditory information about what created this experience, even as the images unfolded before me and as I began to relive the experience in my body.

I saw myself close up, lying on a low altar of what appeared to be a dimly lit alcove of a church. I was full of peace and joy, as this was to be a ceremony in my honor. I was young, maybe sixteen or seventeen, innocent, and feeling trust, peace and a flutter of excitement. Then like in a movie, the camera panned back and I saw I was surrounded by a circle of people wearing black hooded robes. They were standing with their backs to me. While I could not see their faces, I "knew" who they were - my parents, new husband, neighbors, religious and community leaders my father worked with closely.

I "heard" in my head that I had the gift of sight, of clairvoyance. I knew things about my father's secret and corrupt dealings and in my innocence had shared that information the way a child might share a strange dream. I had joked and shared these secrets, not realizing what I would bring down upon myself. I had also known immediately that the place was Salem, Massachusetts, at the time of the witch hysterias. To those gathered, my "gift" was proof of my consorting with Satan.

Then those in the circle turned facing inward. I saw that all the man wore a heavy metal belt at their waist. A dark robed figure stepped forward out of the shadows and then I saw the serrated black steel blade about twelve inches long. It hung erect and I realized in a flash of horror that he intended to rape me with this "rapier" sword. Then the camera panned even further back and I saw I was nine months pregnant. In the grip of terror I realized this was not rape, but murder, intended to kill me and my unborn baby.

I began to cry out and wail, and writhe on the mat. My partner and I were the only two people left in the chapel, all others, including our staff facilitator, had gone to lunch. Finally, my partner caught someone's eye in passing, and they ran to find a staff member. I lay there as the unthinkable was about to unfold for me and my unborn child. My physical body felt as if thousands of needles were being inserted, as waves of stinging heat engulfed me. The staff member arrived and coached me to breathe and come back to present time. My hands and body were buzzing and tingling with energy as I lay sobbing. I couldn't move my body at all for several minutes as it was locked in the tremendous energy release activated by this soul memory.

After lunch, my partner and I reconvened, to continue our work. Exhausted, I lay down hoping for some gentle healing energy to relieve the trauma that had been triggered. But as soon as my partner touched my head, I was right back in the room of horrors. Only this time, I was looking down from above on the bloody scene of myself and my dead baby. I was in emotional and physical agony, clinging to the edge of life and death. This is where a piece of my soul had been trapped in perpetual trauma, unable to break free and return to the Light, until now.

Then I saw myself surrounded by angelic teams and I watched as my soul and that of my baby left their bodies and were both received into the embrace of divine love in the form of etheric angels. I watched and felt as my present day soul healed this past life death trauma that had never been resolved. I journeyed with the mother and child up through a luminous tunnel of golden light, where together we were bathed in light and incredible Love, until I could feel it was time to release the former me and the soul of my baby back to Spirit. I watched as they continued floating further up the tunnel toward a bright white light, escorted by several angelic beings. My partner had continued the illumination process as I completed this experience. I lay quietly for some time unable to speak or move.

This revelation had a huge impact on my psyche and body, the energy of the release was still coursing thru my veins. The healing had soothed me, but the shocking images and events were burned in my brain. It took months to recover and integrate the experience.

I had never delved into past lives for myself, or deliberately sought such experiences. I believed that our soul experienced many lives in its journey. Yet, I'd come to the shamanic classes fully expecting to be clearing out more trauma baggage from this life, which I was doing, but at a much deeper level than I could have imagined. What I would experience thru much of my shamanic healing process and professional training with this school grounded in a Peruvian Lineage, was healing at the SOURCE OR ORIGIN OF MY CORE WOUNDS AND SOUL LOSS. Since I was heeding the call of the shamanic healer, I was also being called to heal to the core of my wounded Rainbow Warrior Soul. Only then would I be able to facilitate others in healing their wounds at their root, and help them reclaim their lost soul essence and power.

Many insights came in the weeks following this healing. First, was the issue of having a "feminine" gift of sight, seeing, and knowing what others wished to keep hidden. I'd been shown this was one of many "natural, intuitive powers" women often had, which with the rise of Christianity had been twisted by church leaders into "the work of the Devil".

Salem Massachusetts was one of the last bastions for the Witchcraft hysteria that had swept through Europe between 1450 and 1700. Between 60,000 and 100,000, (and some sources say many more than that), were executed for "witchcraft". Eighty five percent of those tortured and killed were women.

In 1484, the church launched its official campaign against "witchcraft" with the publication of the authoritative *Witch-Hunter's Manual*, which was re-published thirty times, into the mid seventeenth century. The few remaining volumes depict gruesome scenes of naked women, chained and bound, with swords, spears and other weapons lodged in their hearts, bellies, wombs and eyes, or being burned alive at the stake. Death by torture was prescribed. A gentle death was by hanging. Not all deaths were public spectacles. Many accused women died at home after a "brief illness"; and those who were "carrying a child of Satan", would "die in childbirth". Many heinous crimes against women "witches" would go with them to their graves.

These "witches" were the herbalists, healers, midwives and folk healers. They often were women who lived close to nature and had "a way" with animals. Because they revered nature and communed with helping spirits, or had "magical powers", much as shamans have had for millennia, they were accused of doing the work of the Devil. Because they possessed spiritual and healing powers, they were a threat to the church and the new ways of "medicine" that were emerging. And so the witch hunts were both a cultural genocide and genocide of women's natural feminine gifts, powers and place in the world.

These deep scars still haunt women and much of our world today. Women and the sacred feminine aspects of women and our own life-giving Mother Earth continue to be repressed and violated on a global scale. Current world news events bear witness to the continuing atrocities perpetrated against women of all ages, races and creeds to this day, right alongside the corporate rape of our feminine, life-giving Mother Earth. There are few among us who do not carry these deep soul wounds. For many, they lie forgotten and deeply buried in the subconscious. But for those in whom these wounds continue to create emotional suffering and patterns of trauma, healing is available thru the domains of energy medicine and shamanic healing.

My literal connection to Salem, Massachusetts, made my soul memories all the more visceral. A few years prior, I'd moved from southern New Hampshire to Salem. I lived there for three years, renting a condo only a few blocks from the Salem Witch Museum. Upon moving into my new home, my eating disorder, which had been chronic but manageable, went out of control. I would come home from work, or be home on a weekend, and would eat everything in sight. I'd devour an entire box of crackers with half a jar of peanut butter and then move on to whatever was on hand, which usually included sweets, consumed in their entirety. I'd eat until my stomach hurt, and still the urge to eat overwhelmed all reason or self-control.

I have no doubt it was the horrific soul memory that unconsciously lured me back to Salem, and eventually to a path where the wound could be healed. While I lived in Salem, however, the only way I could "cope" with the activation of this soul energy was through repressing it with food, literally keeping the emotions and the memory of this horror stuffed down and buried deep in my subconscious.

This past life reflected the themes of betrayal that had shadowed me repeatedly in this life. It shed light on a deeper source of my abandonment wound, as those closest to me had participated in the ritualized murder of me and my unborn child. And, I could never stand to hear a baby cry. The sound of a crying baby had always caused stabs of incredible grief in me. And in this lifetime, I was not to have any children of my own.

During the class processing time, our teacher told us how it was not unusual for souls bound by unresolved past life trauma experiences to "find each other" at these trainings so their soul's healing could unfold. That evening, my partner for the healing work and I sat at dinner together sharing more about our current lives. It was then that she revealed she lived in Salem, Massachusetts.

Studying with other healers, and in my practice, I had witnessed several past life healings. It was not unusual for those seeking to claim their medicine ways and healing gifts, to experience tremendous fear, and even stop their studies. I'd had terrible anxiety attacks for many months after beginning my healing practice and had to overcome the irrational fear of "being seen" as a healer. Before long, I was helping facilitate others in healing horrific past life memories of being burned at the stake, publicly tortured, murdered by partners and hanged.

One day, I did healing sessions for three women who were participating in a weekend retreat, a grandmother, mother and daughter. As I cleared each of their energy fields, I discovered all three had the crystalline energies imbedded around their neck from being hanged. These I cleared, along with repairing the throat chakra, and releasing the associated trauma from the energy field. After the session, two of the women told me they'd been having chronic "throat issues", but their doctor had not been able to find anything wrong.

A first time client came to me complaining of severe abdominal pains. She'd been to two doctors, who had run a series of tests, taken x-rays and CAT Scans, but could find nothing wrong. She arrived with her husband, who insisted on staying just outside the healing room in the waiting area during her session. I could see immediately that there were toxic chords binding this couple together. During the session, the woman confided that her husband had been having an affair.

I sat at her head with my hands resting gently at the base of her skull, to assist her in relaxing. In a matter of moments a scene flashed of her in another life time. Her husband in that lifetime, burst through the door in a rage, accusing her of an affair, and that someone else had fathered the child she was carrying. Then he drew a knife, stabbing her repeatedly in the abdomen.

During the session, I cleared her chakras of dense energies, healing the trauma in her energy body, cleared the crystallized energies from the attack, and called in the healing teams that could transform all of this experience back to light, extended that healing to the one who had murdered her in this past life. He was with her again in this lifetime, and was sitting in the waiting room. He was not a murderer in this lifetime. But they remained bound soul to soul by their past.

As we processed our session, I told her what had been cleared through her courage to seek healing. It was then that she told me she'd been having a recurring dream of being murdered by her husband. By clearing the toxic energy field and toxic chords binding this woman to her husband, she would be less likely to continue relating to her husband as the powerless victim in her marriage. But more healing would be needed for permanent healing of these highly toxic wounds.

Finding our voices and power as women remains a huge personal, cultural and global issue. For women as an entire "gender group", half of humanity, have been the target of trauma and repression by those we love and trust and those in power, for millennia. I believe healing this paradigm is one of most urgent callings we have as women and as human beings, if we are to restore balance to our souls, our communities and our planet.

The majority of shamanic healing is done in the "energetic". It's a process of clearing heavy energies, and restoring the natural, much lighter energies, balancing and restoring our system to its highest and aligned natural state of being. Much of the time a client will be deeply relaxed and at peace. A great deal of the "hucha," or heavy energies, and the deepest wounds are cleared energetically, without the need to know the story, or what the energy "means". It simply needs to be cleared. Shamanic practices allow very deep clearings of these unconscious energies, as well as the retrieval of lost soul parts, essential energies for restoring our power and wholeness.

Yet, sometimes the story awakens in us to be seen and re-experienced. I believe this only happens when there is information that is useful or even essential to us on our healing journey. Once the energy of trauma has been cleared and the energy/soul body healed, our stories lose their grip on us; they lose their "charge" and no longer govern how we see ourselves or how we move through the world. Our stories become sources of insight and power; they no longer bind us to the past or to disempowering patterns or beliefs. When we heal to the core of our being, we are able to source our lives from a deep pool of wisdom and grace; we become empowered to live the life we came here to live.

Each of us carries the wisdom of our "indigenous soul" in our DNA. Until very recently in our human history, we lived intimately with animals and nature. We recognized all creation as living energy that carried wisdom. We understood how dependent we were upon the gifts of the earth, the rains, the sun, the moon. We lived cooperatively, mostly in small groups, moving from place to place with the seasons and the food supplies; and we lived in reciprocity with Mother Earth and Creator, giving thanks often for all that was given.

A part of us remembers and is hungry for this connection to the Earth, and the seasons and cycles of nature. There is a deep soul longing for something unnamable. We are children of the Earth; she is our one true mother. Yet many people today feel little, if any, connection to her. Perhaps our deepest soul wound is this loss of our relationship with Mother Earth and our Indigenous Soul.

But when we gaze into the heart of a flower, glimpse a bird on the wing, meander through a forest after the rain, or gaze out across a rolling sea, we are reminded of the love we hold in our hearts for our Mother Earth, and the boundless unconditional love and wonder she offers us every day of our lives. - *Debra Lightheart*

Chapter 20

Mother Earth Calls

*D*uring my multi-year shamanic apprenticeship, I had a series of powerful dreams. One night, I was visited by a large eagle constellation of stars flying over a flowing river of stars. The eagle dove into the river and with its talons retrieved a great salmon star constellation. His eyes were fierce and piercing. As he flew low, directly over my head I heard, "Go to the West. Go to the West."

The next night, in my dream, I saw myself standing on a large boulder overlooking a vast expanse of land and sky. Again, I was told I had a mission to do in the West.

I heard myself ask, "What if I don't go?" I immediately saw the sky turn blood red as if it were on fire. As I scanned the horizon, there were massive explosions and fires everywhere. The images were haunting and frightening. I couldn't get them or the words, "Go to the West", out of my mind.

In a matter of months, my life in Maine unraveled, I packed my car and drove west to Santa Fe, New Mexico.

A short while after my arrival, I met a woman at a small gathering. As we began to talk, it was clear we had ceremonial work to do together. She'd had a dream that someone would be coming to work with her to facilitate Earth healing ceremonies in the area. As it so happened, I had brought with me a number of replica Inca Sun staffs, blessed by the Inca Q'ero medicine men and women of the high Andes. A group of their students had been placing these Earth acupuncture needles strategically around the planet as guided by Spirit and the lineages of Earth Keepers. I'd felt deeply called to participate, and had acquired the brass "staffs", not knowing at the time when or where I would be called to use them.

Soon after meeting my partner for this work, another dream revealed the pattern of the grid we would create. My partner and I spread out a map of the region and began to lay out our plan of where to begin our series of Earth ceremonies. For the better part of a year, we carried out our work, each site calling for its own process and ceremony. We knew our ceremonies had significance, given the circumstances and locations we'd been called to conduct our work.

We placed the last staff at the central point of our work on Thanksgiving Day. I closed my eyes to tune into the moment, asking for guidance, protection and "invisibility" as we set about this final ceremony. Immediately, I felt the presence of Don Manuel Q'espi who had passed over a few years prior. Don Manuel was the elder and most powerful medicine healer of the Peruvian Q'ero at the time of his passing. Though I did not know him personally, I'd been initiated into his lineage as I received my shamanic rites. I immediately recognized his spiritual presence, and great love flooded my being as tears streamed down my cheeks. I felt our work was being validated and supported, though we knew only our part of a much larger process unfolding across the region and the planet.

Three years later, northern New Mexico had a raging fire season, one lapping at the edges of the Los Alamos Nuclear Lab. This was the second fire to threaten that area in less than a decade. The first fire had ravaged portions of the town. Now as residents were again being evacuated, it seemed disaster was at hand. Political leaders assured us through the news media that there was no threat, even as tons of nuclear related waste material was stored in tents near the perimeter of the fire, to say nothing of the hazards that lay behind locked gates, surveillance cameras and razor wire.

I monitored the progress of the fires that summer and could only wonder at the potential disaster licking at the gates of the Los Alamos Nuclear Lab compound and the entire mesa overlooking the region's largest water supply, the Rio Grande River. It was surreal to watch the flames at night, knowing that should the fire continue to move in a deadly direction, it could ignite a nuclear fire cloud of contamination.

As I watched the red sky and the shooting flames of fire, I recalled the compelling dreams that brought me to Santa Fe, the Earth ceremonies and Don Q'espi's spiritual presence. I prayed that all the spiritual forces working with and through the Earth Keepers would keep this region and our planet safe from a nuclear disaster. The fire did change course, by just a few miles, devastating the forests and water shed of the neighboring Santa Clara Pueblo, home to members of the Native American Tewa tribe. It will take decades for their people and their lands to recover. A nuclear fire cloud was avoided, but at great cost.

During my shamanic training, I felt the need to deeply immerse myself not just in nature, but in wilderness. When I was about to turn fifty, I decided this would be the time to honor myself and my journey with an experience where I could tap into my inner "wild woman". A well-known teacher of Native American lineage would be facilitating our week-long wilderness experience on sacred ground in Wolf Creek, Montana.

The medicine bowl landscape was spectacular, with rolling wild flower meadows and steep mountains surrounding a pristine valley, carved through its depths by a crystal clear stream. The presence of the ancestors was palpable, and the land featured ancient medicine wheels, eagle catch pits and burial sites. This was sacred ground. Deep within the belly of this region, was a series of caves. When re-discovered by the current ranch owners, decades earlier, a bear and a bison skull were still resting on the ceremonial altars, deep in the womb of mother Earth. This had been a gathering place of ceremony and trade; buffalo had thrived here and died here. The place resonated into my bones, and spoke to my indigenous soul.

Despite the warnings about grizzlies, and cougars, I felt right at home in the wilderness. I was "fearless" in this environment; in fact, I'd never felt more alive and nourished. That is not to say I was not mindful of my surroundings, and the animals whose domain I ventured upon.

One day of the retreat was dedicated to a solo "meditation or visioning" sun up to sunset, in a place of our choosing. Water and food, cameras, notebooks, etc. were to be left behind so we could be fully nourished by the raw wilderness, without distraction. The day dawned, a chilly forty degrees with a brisk wind whipping across the valley. I was grateful I had brought enough layers, but knew I would have to find a place out of the wind for the hours of sitting. As I wandered the landscape, I came within a few feet of a doe and her fawn, and saw the telltale signs of bear scratched on a tree and in rocks that had been overturned in search of insects.

I meandered across the landscape drinking it in through all my senses. Then I saw the pair of robins. I followed their flight with my eyes to a nearby tree, and there was my place; a ledge out cropping that dropped below the ridge, out of the wind and facing the sun. It was warm, safe and quiet with an expansive view of the valley below in three directions.

I created my sacred space to sit and commune with my spirit and nature, open to what messages I would receive. I set my intention to meet a spirit helper for my healing journey. I sat watching the ants at work on the edges of my circle and the pair of robins tending their young. Time passed. My thoughts and spirit wandered.

A huge golden eagle flew by below me in the valley, his massive wings outstretched as he confidently rode the strong current of wind. In the afternoon, movement caught my eye as two elk trotted off away from me, perhaps having caught my scent. I followed their movement as they faded into the distance. As my eyes refocused, I realized the entire meadow of one mountainside was in motion as a large elk herd, including many calves, grazed on the impossibly steep slopes.

As the drum called us back at dusk, I reluctantly closed my circle and began the walk back to camp. As I rounded the last curve of hill, I could see in the distance something moving….it was cream colored…and moving at a slow jog….I couldn't make out if it was a dog….it was too big for a cat….and the color didn't match with anything I could conjure up in my mind.

I eased my pace and stayed out of view as best I could…..and then it turned and looked right at me….it's yellow eyes….indifferent…but steady. It was a bobcat, not albino, but buff white, its stub of a tail and large paws visible even at distance. I held my breath until it trotted on down the path and disappeared into the brush. I found its large tracks along the edge of the stream. My request for a helping spirit had been answered; and for a time, bobcat medicine would assist me on my healing journey.

The next day, we prepared to visit the ancient caves. I shuttered with excitement and reverence that I would be entering the caves used by ancient ones and American Indian tribes for millennia, a sacred holy place to honor Mother Earth and Creator. Once we crept passed the entrance we were immersed in total blackness, until we turned on our head lamps to make our way over the slippery rocks, deep into the caves which stretched five miles into the heart of the valley above. Something deep within me stirred, like a forgotten dream. I knew I had been here before.

We gathered around the ancient stone altar in silence. Turning off our headlamps, we were held for a time in the deep, dark womb of Mother Earth; our breath mingling with hers in the velvet darkness. Softly, our offerings of song pierced the profound silence, punctuated by the drip, drip, drip, of water finding its way into the belly of the cave. I began to tone with sounds, and for half an hour our group wove wave after wave of heartfelt sounds and prayers, joining all those that had reverberated across time from this sacred place. It was a holy place and a holy time. We emerged into the shining day of the medicine bowl valley; each one of us glowing with the inner light awakened from the depths of our souls, and our profound reunion with our one true Mother.

Integration from my first wilderness experience continued for several weeks upon my return home to Maine. I received my first "spirit name" I'd been questing for; songs and healing chants in ancient languages began to flow through me and became part of my healing "medicine". Bobcat guided me through a chapter of my healing journey. My Montana experience would be the first of several shamanic wilderness retreats; each offering profound blessings and powerful gifts.

We may reach times in our healing journey where we've had "enough"! We simply are tired of having to look at an issue one more time, or process yet another painful experience. We want to be "done" with our healing. And we will reach that place in our own way, in our own time. We often heal our wounds in ever deepening layers. It's important to remember that with each piece of our healing, we are also reclaiming more of our power!

Since our healing is also our path to empowerment, we can embrace our journey from a different perspective. Rather than feeling trapped as a victim who will never be healed, we can see ourselves as the courageous warrior who is reclaiming more and more of our authentic power, wisdom and personal truth. Every act of healing is an act of self-empowerment and a powerful step on the path of our soul's evolution. — *Debra LighHeart*

Chapter 21

Healing the Rainbow Soul

Shortly after the Montana retreat, I resumed my shamanic training. The first day, our teacher led us on two shamanic journeys; the first was to a life time where we had been deeply aligned with our authentic spiritual power and soul purpose.

I readily followed the call of the rattle and the monotone voice of the teacher. Soon I found myself in a much earlier time and place. I was priestess and steward of the surrounding sacred groves and springs. I lived with my extended family on a beautiful and peaceful sanctuary where I was the high priestess of a mystery school, apprenticing others in the sacred arts of healing, magic and honoring of the sacred feminine and Mother Earth. I was full of life, love and light; fully engaged in my soul's purpose, and surrounded by loving family. I could feel the expansiveness of my heart and energy field as my life and my soul's purpose were being fully expressed. It was an incredible feeling, and I was reluctant to return when the teacher called us back.

On the second journey, we were instructed to be shown a life time where we had lost or abused our power. As I journeyed, I was confused, for I had returned to the same lifetime as before. But then, within moments, I began to smell smoke and see flames in the distance. I "knew" it was the invading Roman armies, raping and pillaging their way across the landscape, gathering up all those who had not submitted to Roman rule. Soon the army was amassed in our lands, and in a matter of minutes, my life, as I'd known it, was over.

The sacred groves were set on fire; my parents and elderly grandparents were slain before my eyes. My husband and I, carrying my young son, less than a year old, were put in chains, joining neighbors and those from nearby villages on a forced march into slavery. On the way, as my son cried out in thirst and fear, a soldier grabbed him from my arms, swung him around by his feet, smashing his head on a rock, leaving him like trash by the road; my husband though chained, had tried to intervene, and was swiftly killed on the spot. By the time we reached the city, we were filthy, thirsty and starving. I was numb with grief, shock and exhaustion.

I was thrown into a muddy old pig sty. My dress was tattered and torn, barely offering any coverage for my body. I was weak with hunger and thirst, and seared with the grief of losing all those I loved, and the destruction of the sacred groves. I lay weeping in exhaustion, and disbelief of my circumstances, praying to the Divine Mother for a quick and merciful death.

Four Roman soldiers making their rounds saw me lying there, and began to approach. I thought they might offer me some water or a crust of bread. But instead, they began making leering and obscene gestures my way. Then they approached, entered the pen, and one by one set about raping me. I was too weak to fight or cry out. I saw that in the process of this ordeal, I died. We were called back to the room by the teacher and his rattle, and I sat numb at what I'd been shown, as the reawakened energies of this trauma coursed through my body.

Once again, it took weeks to integrate from the session, and again, I knew this life time had been shown to me for a reason. It revealed much about my core patterns, traumas and issues in this life that could only be healed fully from the perspective of the soul. I also knew that a part of my soul was still caught in this drama. I would need to release this aspect of my being back to the Light, and restore the soul essence that had been lost. I would need to heal old contracts and beliefs that had formed as a result of this horrific soul trauma.

The most striking realization from the two journeys was that the lifetime when I was most in my authentic power also became the lifetime where I completely lost my power, and my trust in Spirit. That shadow wound, had been tracking me for a very long time, and ran deeply through my present lifetime.

Since childhood, I'd been displaced repeatedly. I'd lost home after home, many that were "true sanctuaries for my soul". As an adult, again and again, as I reached for my "dream" or started toward a desired goal or outcome, things have fallen apart. Doorways to new opportunities closed just as I was about to enter; sources of support dried up at critical times; plans have gone awry in perfect timing to derail my momentum. The pattern of chronic loss and derailment of momentum toward my highest aspirations plagued my adult life, leaving me feeling frustrated and discouraged.

Eventually, I would find a gifted healer who recognized immediately that I had a "pattern of protection" imbedded in my energy field. This pattern was attempting to protect me from the "annihilation" I had experienced in other lifetimes, for being "seen", for being "successful", for being in my power, or stepping outside the acceptable norm of the times. The healer told me that IF I had fully achieved the level of power I was capable of in this life, prior to clearing this pattern; the devastation would have quickly followed as it had done before. The two patterns of being in my power, and being destroyed when I was in my power, were woven tightly together as one. I gladly gave her permission to clear that pattern and several others that were still actively disrupting my present day life, although their origins were many lifetimes ago.

Among the lingering patterns was my abandonment issue. Although I'd done work around this previously, I was still bound to the abandonment energy through my unrelenting guilt, and belief that I was the "cause" of my parents and others having abandoned me. During a week of soul retrieval training, my classmates and I all delved deeply to heal our soul wounds and reclaim sources of our power. My partner had retrieved several soul parts, and now I was doing the integration work of fully reclaiming these soul parts.

She had brought back two small children, a brother and sister who were twins. I wanted to know who they were, and where their mother was. I lay down and stepped into the energy of the little girl as my partner asked my questions. "Who are you? Why are you here?"

As I lay on my side, a childlike voice replied, "Our mother left us here to be safe. She said she'd come back for us, but she never did. We're afraid and alone. We want our mother."

I began to sob in recognition of this soul truth. I "saw" how I'd been caught up in a roundup of our villagers, for defying the local land baron in some way. I had hidden the children in a hollow at the bottom of a long hill below the village, in what I hoped would be a safe place until I returned under the cover of night. But I'd been caught along with most of the villagers in the turmoil and raiding of our village and was taken by wagon many miles from my home and my children, never to see them again.

I had lived the rest of my short life in agony for having abandoned my children, and I'd never forgiven myself for it. What I'd set in motion for my soul, was continued "punishment" for abandoning my children. And so I'd created a pattern of abandonment, knowingly or unknowingly, it didn't really matter. Both had the effect of re-wounding my soul, until I was willing and able to change this form of self-abuse and core beliefs that I deserved to be punished, and abandoned.

These children were not only my lost children, but lost parts of me. I needed to bless and release them back to Spirit, and bless and forgive myself. I would also need to clear and re-write old soul contracts keeping me bound to this wound of the past. This insight into my soul's history was a huge revelation for me, as I'd suffered greatly from the many times I'd been abandoned in this life time. The realization that I had indeed previously abandoned my own children, provided the starting point for healing this core wound and the pattern of suffering it wove through my life.

During my shamanic training, I was introduced early on to the concept of self-sorcery, and I began to see how much I abused myself through my negative beliefs, thoughts, and behaviors. I was my own sharp critic and judge, having taken on these behaviors early in childhood. Our shamanic practices revealed how the energy and power of thoughts and words affected our energy body, and those on whom we projected these energies. As our training continued in healing the shadow, we learned processes for extracting dense energies imbedded in the energy field that were impacting our lives. We learned firsthand how the "projection" of our shadow on to ourselves or others, by our judgments, anger, or jealousy can become imbedded in the energy field, and our physical body.

No matter how advanced in their education, spiritual development or what background and circumstances, everyone in the shamanic training had these energies in their luminous energy field. Some were in crystal form and some were in fluid form. In some cases entities or spirits that had lost their way had become attached. Many of us were carrying energies which had been imbedded in the luminous energy field of our soul for many lifetimes. None of the sixty or more shamanic healing students was exempt from carrying these energies, but all were committed to their removal.

In this Peruvian lineage medicine path, energy is viewed as either heavy or light. The medicine teachers of this lineage do not judge the energy as "good" or "bad", simply whether or not it is serving our highest good. Modern medicine does not recognize energy intrusions, and cannot treat afflicted individuals, except by attempting to treat "symptoms" with drugs. But only the removal of these intrusive energies can bring any real and permanent relief. Extraction of intrusive energies is a core shamanic healing practice that often brings immediate relief to suffering individuals. However, one must be well along in their own healing and shamanic practice to do this work without causing further harm to their client or themselves.

Those who have suffered trauma, often experience soul loss and are highly likely to have intrusive energies. These energy field "imprints" attract more of the same kind of energy to them. This, combined with soul loss, can leave a person a virtual magnet for further trauma and abuse. The accumulation of these energies, and "the hole in the soul" left from trauma, often leads to depression, mental health disorders, addictions, and/ or chronic illness. The healing and repair of the luminous energy body or "soul", including the removal of intrusive energies and retrieval of lost soul parts, is essential to restoring health and well-being especially where there has been significant trauma. Some of these energies may be generational patterns that are deeply imbedded and repeated until cleared at the level of pure energy and spirit....the domain of the shamanic healer.

From the shamanic perspective, dis-ease has a spiritual foundation accompanied by underlying imbalances in the body's energy system and luminous energy field. These imbalances are often accompanied by distorted belief systems, and "soul contracts" deeply rooted in the subconscious. Often these discordant energy patterns and beliefs are passed generation to generation. The shaman is trained how to access these domains of the energy body and soul, with the permission of the client. Here are not only our soul wounds, but the lost or displaced sources of our power, waiting to be reclaimed; quanta of energy which can help restore our soul to wholeness. Through the realms of shamanic healing, where an individual has been power-less, they become power-full.

We are being called to awaken and align with the Truth of who we are, and who we are becoming as the Luminous Ones, the Humans of the Light. It has taken thousands of years to reach this time in our evolution, yet we have carried the seeds of light within us always. They have lain dormant a long time, amidst the trials and turmoil across the ages of human history. Each one of us carries that history, as well as the Codes of Light that, when activated, awaken this dormant aspect of our DNA and our God Brain.

The Ancient Ones, the Ascended Emissaries of Light, and the Wisdom Keepers throughout time have carried this knowing for us through the centuries. Now, a great collective of souls is gathering around the globe - in circles, in ceremonies, on pilgrimage - to help birth this new fully conscious human. Because the time of the "Great Shift" is at hand, the healing, the letting go, the awakening process is moving at lightning speed compared to the past.

The activation of the Codes of Light through rites and ceremonies infuses our healing capacities to new heights. Wounds which bound us to suffering, simply fall away from our awareness, or are readily cleared and released. Through the gifting of sacred rites, dormant neural pathways are activated, sparking our consciousness to awaken, so our vision and actions are guided by our hearts, rather than our ego or fear.   *- Debra LightHeart*

Chapter 22

Healing Beyond Death

*T*he shamanic healer travels between worlds and into other realms of consciousness to access healing powers and wisdom, and to help bring healing to the living as well as those souls who have passed over. Death is not viewed as an end point, but rather a transition, and time of rest until the next cycle of rebirth and spiritual lessons. Since the soul and spirit is eternal, the shamanic healer learns how to tend to the soul, whether in the physical body or in the realms of spirit. Knowing how to die, how to exit the physical body at the time of death, and being able to assist a dying person in making their spirit flight, is one of the many practices a shaman can offer those in their community. For millennia, shamans have been the midwives of the soul.

And so, one of our tasks as shamanic apprentices was to journey to a loved one that had passed over, one we believed might be caught in one of the lower levels of the upper world, on their way back to Spirit.

The majority of souls return to the Light and the company of their ancestors. But if one dies with a great deal of heavy "hucha" energy, then clearing must take place before the soul can complete its journey back to the Light.

I knew immediately I wanted to check on June's status. I had the feeling that she had died with so much heavy energy in her being, that she might not have completed her full journey back to Spirit. I journeyed to the upper world as instructed, and found her in the plant kingdom. She was simply sitting on a bench among the green plants, unaware of my presence. I returned from my shamanic journey with a clear purpose in mind, if June wished to participate. We were learning a process to call back the energy body of one who had not completed their transition. We would each take a turn being the shaman, and being the "surrogate" body, giving the energy bodies a temporary place to land for this rapid and transformative healing. As usual, we had counted off by number. None of us had ever met before.

I would be witness to the work, as one student lay on the massage table to be the surrogate to receive June's light body. I would have a minute or two to dialogue with June's essence if I wished, as the clearing was taking place. The practicing shaman journeyed to June's soul essence, and received permission to proceed with the clearing.

The presence of June's energy was heavy, and sticky. The shamanic student worked quickly, and we could all feel the shift to much lighter energies on the table. I thanked June for all that she had given me in this life, and wished her release from all her suffering. Then it was time for her to be escorted all the way back to Spirit and the place of the ancestors. There was a rush of energy and even joy as she departed. As we processed the experience, the shamanic apprentice who had escorted June back to the place of the ancestors said to me, "Oh, one more thing. There was a man with a full head of white hair there to greet her. I don't know if this means anything to you or not, but I felt I should tell you."

It meant a great deal to me, as tears sprang to my eyes. Snowie! Snowie was there to welcome June back to the realm of Spirit. The circle for their life's journey was now complete and brought me a greater sense of peace and closure. And it was deeply powerful to learn the kind of energy healing that can alleviate suffering, even for those "beyond the veil".

Ceremony and initiation rites played a central role during my shamanic healing and practitioner training. It was essential to continuously clear and repair my energy field in order to step more and more into my power. Fire and despacho ceremonies are an integral part of growing our medicine as shamanic healers stepping into this ancient Peruvian Lineage. Fire has the power of rapid transformation, as it quickly consumes heavy energies. The shamanic path I was walking was the path of fire.

The art of the Despacho Ceremony is a path unto itself. With great care and intention, offerings are created in a sacred way, wrapped, and burned in a ceremonial fire. The Q'ero shamans have some two hundred versions of this one ceremony, including those to help the patient to heal, be cured of illness, to manifest abundance or to reverse curses and bad luck. They are also prepared frequently as offerings to Pacha Mama, Mother Earth, to maintain or restore balance. Masters of the Despacho Ceremony are rightfully considered powerful healers. Such ceremonies engage the spiritual realms and the creative life force energies which exist outside of time; they can benefit the living as well as those whose souls have crossed over to other dimensions. Ceremonies are central to all "shamanistic" practices, and are the source of much of the shaman's healing powers.

The most precious gift the Q'ero medicine people of the Andes have offered us in the West is the gift of the "karpays". These energetic rites of luminous energies help awaken the innate wisdom of the rainbow soul or luminous body. These Seeds of Light are now being shared at this time to assist with the great spiritual awakening on our planet.

I had received these rites during my shamanic apprenticeship, and was drawn immediately to learning how to transmit them to others. So I journeyed from Maine to Joshua Tree, California were three of the Q'ero Shamans from Peru would be personally sharing these sacred rites and ceremonies. We would be learning the new form of the rites, now called the Munay-Ki Rites of Enlightenment; Munay-Ki, meaning Love in Motion.

It is the heartfelt wish of these gentle but powerful Wisdom Keepers and Earth Keepers that these seeds of light be shared for the benefit of humanity and Pacha Mama, our Mother Earth. Their ancient prophecies speak of the time of the Pachacuti, when the world would be turned upside down. These medicine people know this time has come by the many dramatic shifts now occurring on the Pacha Mama herself: the receding of the glaciers in the high Andes (and worldwide), numerous earthquakes and volcanic eruptions, floods, droughts, massive wild fires, changing weather patterns, and what is now being called "the fifth great extinction", as loss of species escalates to numbers known only to occur during four other cataclysmic times on Earth.

These "changing of the times" are calling for a rapid evolution of the human heart and spirit away from fear and greed, toward love and gratitude; from confrontation to cooperation; from reactive decisions, to proactive vision. To make such a change, we as humans need to literally "upload" a new energetic operating system; one that brings us into alignment with Source, our planet, and our human destiny. The role of the Wisdom Keepers and their medicine gifts is to help the Earth and humanity not only successfully transition through such times, but to evolve. Whether we realize it or not, many of us are here on Earth at this time to help facilitate this shift in consciousness. Many resources are available to assist us in this evolutionary process to literally activate the soul, and manifest a new dream for humanity and our world.

The Munay-Ki rites are offered as "seeds" of potential that each recipient is responsible for growing in his or her own soul. The first seeds are powerful archetypal energies planted in each chakra. The rites also connect the recipient to lineages of Healers, Day Keepers, Wisdom Keepers, Earth Keepers, and to the stars and all creation. There are rites to awaken the ability to "see through the heart"; and bands of power, offering protection and transmutation of heavy energies that come our way. All the rites are fed with fire; much the way a seed planted in the earth needs not only nourishing soil and water, but the sun's fire. These rites heal our luminous body and awaken our latent potentials as spiritual beings. They are gently and powerfully transformative.

During the Munay-Ki initiation week, we learned to feed the energies of the rites and awaken their potential within ourselves as we created new ceremonies for each. The Q'ero joyfully engaged with those gathered across language and culture, and delighted in the new expressions of these energies thousands of miles from their home in the Peruvian Andes. Later in the week, a personal *despacho,* (prayer bundle) prepared by the most senior and powerful Q'ero elder, opened a wave of energy that carried me through much of that year. There's was a journey of extraordinary generosity and vision, in keeping with the prophecies their lineage had carried for hundreds, if not thousands of years.

By the end of the retreat, we were all filled with so much love and light! Just being in the energy field of these mystical medicine men and women made me feel "drunk" from their high vibrational energies. I left feeling lighter and more expansive than ever before. And when I returned home without any publicity at all, calls began coming in from retreat centers requesting the *Munay-Ki rites*, retreats, classes and healing sessions. I knew the blessings of Don Umberto's despacho, as well as the rites growing in me, were carrying me forward on my true path. And, like all those walking the shamanic path before me, my task would be to walk with a foot in both worlds (the ordinary and non-ordinary realities), and not get lost or bound to either one.

Chapter 23

Fire Walker

*T*he truth is we are far more than we've been led to believe. I chose to participate in a fire walk to remind myself of this during a difficult life transition.

I arrived at the ceremonial location on a cold December night. The snow lay glistening in the moonlight, and the small parking lot was full to overflowing. People were already gathered around the ceremonial fire location, where about a half a cord of wood was stacked in a large formation that assured a hot and thorough burn in about two hours.

The leader of the fire walk opened the evening's ceremony and torched the wood. Soon the blaze was radiating so much heat we had to step back as we watched the flames leaping to the stars. The beating of a drum called us inside, where we would prepare ourselves for the fire walk to come.

As with so many things in life, overcoming fear is the biggest challenge. A room of about thirty people from ages fifteen to eighty-five had come to do just that. With little fanfare our instructor introduced the first exercise designed to help us break through our fear and into a new realm of possibilities. He produced a one inch thick piece of rough wood, laid it across some cinder blocks forming a bridge with the wood. He stood quietly for a few moments, and then with a swift movement brought his hand to the board with enough force that it broke cleanly in two. Wow! We were all impressed! He then placed another piece of wood on the blocks, then motioned for me to come on up. I knew I shouldn't have sat in the front row!

The instructor showed me how to use the base of my palm as the point of contact. He had me hit his hand several times until I had demonstrated the energy he knew by experience it would take to break the board. Then he gestured me toward the "shrine of fear". I stood eyeing the board. When the demonstration began, I was pretty sure I wouldn't be able to perform such a feat. My hands were no longer strong from barn chores, and I was pretty sure it would hurt like Hell to whack my hand on that rough board!

But I refocused my thoughts as I stood confronting the board. I knew the only way I would succeed was to see beyond the board to the other side. If I focused on the surface of the board I would fail. If I focused my energies to break through the board, I would succeed. We were also encouraged to use the board as a metaphor for those things in life from which we were seeking to break free. I called up in my mind all those things I wanted to be free of now! When I had focused my mind and intent, I struck the board. It broke cleanly in two! I raised both arms in exultation, shouting out the energy of the moment, to a room full of applause. Then, one by one, each person came forward to reclaim more of who we all are truly meant to be - masters of our energy.

The next exercise was a trust fall. One by one we were to fall backwards several feet into the catch net of the hands and arms of our companions. There were enough of us that we wove a safety net, and no one carried too much weight, though this would not be recommended for anyone with a back problem! Catching each other was a way to quickly build connection and trust in our group, which would help create a stronger energy field container for the fire walk to come.

For our third "test", we were each presented with an authentic hunting arrow. It was about twenty four inches long, solid wood, and had a tapered, smooth metal tipped point. The instructor demonstrated the exercise twice before setting us loose.

We were to find a place along the wall, placing the flat end of the arrow against the wall and pressing the pointed end of the arrow at the base of our throat, just above the notch in the collar bone. Then when we had focused our energies and intention, we were to press forward into the arrow until it arched and broke.

It was me, the wall, the arrow at my throat and my fear. One by one, I heard others snap their arrows and the round of cheers, while I tried repeatedly, and failed. The arrow point pressed to my throat was sharply painful, and it was scary to think about the possibility of it piercing my throat. I had several close successes, but hadn't summoned the will to break through the pain and the pressure on my throat. I knew we were nearing the time for the fire walk. Finally, I summoned up all the focused determination and intent I could muster, gritted my teeth and went for it. At last! The arrow snapped in two as I sighed in relief, rubbing the sore place at the base of my throat.

With each test, I felt my sense of empowerment grow. Each of us was making an individual and collective shift in our energy fields and our consciousness. As we moved through each exercise, we were moving deeper and deeper into a zone of possibilities that were greater than the ones we usually summoned in our daily lives. We were also weaving an energetic container that was stronger than any of us could hold individually. We were tapping into that zone known to athletes, yogi masters and others, where physical feats are performed that defy logic and stretch our understanding of reality.

Finally, it was time to venture out into the cold night air. We removed our shoes and socks and stood with bare feet in the snow, around what remained of the fire. The leader had raked the coals out into a rectangle about five feet wide, fifteen feet long and several inches deep. Though they had a coating of ash, the coals gleamed with deep orange as they lay spread on the frozen ground. We were given some brief instructions about do's and don'ts for walking the coals. A few drums began a rhythmic beat, while each side of the fire was lined with brave and barefoot souls, faces beaming radiantly in anticipation.

Someone who had participated in several fire walks was the first to go. Then a slow procession followed as cheers went up for each one. Then I felt the tug in my solar plexus that it was time for me to cross the coals. I waited at one end, arms extended at my side, hands cupped up at the moon. Totally unafraid, I walked flat footed across the length of coals, greeted by cheers, and feeling my own spirit soar. I walked three more times before the coals died down. I had crossed through my fears and broken through barriers both internal and external. Everyone walked at least once. To be honest, the most physically uncomfortable aspect of the entire evening was standing in the snow in my bare feet; the frozen snow burned far more than any coals that night! The next day, the souls of my feet were rosy pink, but I didn't have a single blister.

I keep the broken arrow where I can see it and be reminded that I can achieve the impossible. I can break through my own barriers and fears. I can walk in beauty and grace through the fires of life.

(Note to the reader: The fire walk exercises described here should not be attempted without the assistance of a trained professional, in the context of a facilitated "transpersonal" experience.)

Chapter 24

Infinite Bliss

*D*uring my shamanic training, I was invited to join a wilderness retreat in Haines, Alaska. The offer was from the leader of a ceremonial music group that gathered in wilderness settings, to create improvisational, shamanic trance music. I had met the leader during my week in Montana. I'd been on two extraordinary wilderness retreats with this small band of shamanic musicians in Mt. Hood, Oregon and the Wasatch Mountains of Utah. But Alaska would surpass all my imaginings.

Our small group of five musicians arrived in Haines by bush plane, flying in low over the pale green glacial ice. We were then air boated up to a remote peninsula on the confluence of the Chilkat and Chilkoot Rivers, amidst the sparkling splendor and chill of early October. Haines is especially known as a gathering place for Bald Eagles that congregate by the hundreds on her shores for the winter. We were hoping to see some of the early arrivals who would be feasting on the tail end of the fall salmon run.

On our drive through Haines, we pulled over when we spotted hundreds of birds and a few bears feasting. When we opened the car doors, the stench of rotting fish was overwhelming. Across the river, three bears were lolling about half sitting up, clearly satiated from their salmon feast. The energy of the Alaskan wilderness felt crystalline compared to any place I'd ever been in the lower forty-eight states. The raw wildness of the place made me feel more alive than ever before, as all senses were fully stimulated and awake!

It took several trips by airboat to land all our gear – a large assortment of musical instruments, including numerous large drums; ceremonial items, recording equipment, camping gear, and food and water for a week. We set up camp on a large expanse of river flats, surrounded by golden aspen, the frigid glacial waters and snow-capped peaks.

We pitched our tents along the river and formed our ceremonial circle and fire pit, hanging our food high up in a sturdy tree, a considerable distance away, to avoid tempting bears into our camp. We also set about gathering the generous amounts of drift wood we would need for our ceremonial fire and for warmth once the sun set early behind the surrounding mountains. The arrival and set up was an ordeal, with night fall coming on fast, and bears about, though we surmised their bellies were gorged full with salmon.

That evening I prepared dinner, kneeling on the cold river stones, my head lamp a mere pin prick in the dark. Our make shift kitchen was well away from the comfort and safety of the fire. I felt twinges of fear crawl like centipedes up my back as I peered into the black wall of night beyond my small circle of light. My companions sat on the other side of the cavernous darkness, barely audible as their shadows danced around the flickering flames. I clanged the pots, pans and cooking utensils loudly, letting the bears know of our presence; plenty of salmon or not, we were in their territory.

Late that night, as we gathered around our sacred fire, and the drummers drummed, I began to hear the words of a chant and to tentatively sing the words ringing in my head, "I'm a bad ass bear....I'm a bad ass bear".....I could feel the power of this huge bear in my being. But none of us wanted to offend the bears or bear spirit, so we changed the words to *medicine bear* and gave praise to the great medicine bears of this region, and our own spirit bear medicine.

Our chant rose to the heavens as the drums rolled out like thunder. We hoped our prayers would be well received along with our presence. That night, walking back to my tent in the inky darkness, I rang Tibetan chimes to alert the bears of my presence, though I have no doubt they knew exactly where I was and where I was heading.

The night air by the river was damp and cold, with temperatures well below freezing. Tenting so close to the water had not been a good idea, but I was too exhausted to consider moving my campsite, or leaving my few companions. I hardly slept as the chill went to my bones despite all the layers I wore inside my sleeping bag. The hot stone I'd brought from the fire had grown cold, and I lay tossing and shivering, waiting for the dawn.

In the wee hours of the morning, I heard the high pitched moaning of the wind; but no, it wasn't the wind....it was a lone wolf. Her long, thin howl repeating across the vast landscape sent an even deeper chill through my bones....not of fear...but of recognition....of connection to something primal within me. I felt the hair rise on the back of my neck, and I wanted to go out and howl with her. But instead, I listened to her solo song for the remainder of my fitful night's sleep.

The next morning, about ten feet from my tent, was a large mound of purple bear scat and a pattern of tracks passing right by my tent and through our camp site. Another chill coursed through my body. I'd never felt so alive, or perhaps so close to death. This bear had gorged herself on berries as well as salmon, and left her calling card as a reminder. This was her domain. I was grateful we had sung our medicine bear song the night before, to honor the long kinship between bears and humans as spiritual allies. I also made extra sure my canister of certified bear pepper spray remained close at hand.

One afternoon, three members of our clan decided to go salmon fishing, though it was hardly fishing. The salmon were swimming up the glacial streams to take their last gasps of breath, having completed an incredible journey to spawn another generation of their species.

From these shallows, my companions scooped up two large coho salmon with a fishing net. That night we feasted on fresh salmon roasted over the hot coals of our fire, until we too, like the bears, couldn't eat another bite. The guts and remains were taken about a half mile down river and deposited for the wild critters to eat.

That night I could feel the salmon swimming in my blood.....the raw energy of the salmon was literally coursing through my veins. It's no wonder that night around the fire, the chant that came through me during our ceremonial music, honored the salmon, and their place in circle of life in Alaska:

Run Salmon, Run! Run, Salmon Run!
Spawning in the river of life.
Food for the wolf and food for the bear;
Food for the native people living there.
Run salmon run! Run salmon run!
Spawning in the River of Life....River of Life... Run Salmon Run!

The next day, walking along the river beach, I came to a set of boot tracks leading to the water's edge where the fish guts had been deposited.....and right alongside the boot tracks....those of a wolf....and a large bear.

It was our final night in Alaska that would bring a soul experience like no other. We had been drumming and singing around our ceremonial fire for several hours....it was well past midnight....as the drums reverberated I began an improvisational chant....calling to the Ancestors....

Come, Ancestors Come! Bring your Light! Bring your Love!
Come, Ancestors Come!"
Ancient Ones, Come… to our circle, to our sacred fire!
Come, ancestors, come! Bring Your Light! Bring Your Love!
Come ancestors come!

The chant repeated again and again. Chanting and drumming for several hours had already induced a deep trance state. I was lost in the energy of the moment, the immense canopy of stars, the crackling of the fire as it cast our dancing shadows to the edge of the inky darkness outside our circle. The drums were calling, calling, and my chant was repeating over and over.

I began to feel a rush of energy and an incredible lightness. Then I felt a presence within me. Within moments, I was filled with an intense and complete state of bliss, and the incredible feeling of oneness with the universe….a total expansive joy. As this feeling took over my senses, I began to speak in another language, that of an ancient grandmother. She offered her message of love and gratitude, addressing each member of the circle. I was filled with such bliss, tears of joy rolled down my cheeks, as grandmother spoke her blessings.

The leader of our group grew increasingly unnerved by this turn of events, and he finally addressed me by my spirit name, instructing me to "Come back! Come back!" I was present…I was not "out of it". I was fully present to the fact that I was temporarily home to an enlightened ancestor spirit who had heard our prayers and who had come. And I was open enough for her to use my body as a vessel to address and bless each one. As my consciousness shifted to the call back, she quickly departed, along with the expanded awareness she had brought with her.

I had stepped outside of time. I had tasted infinity and the bliss of oneness with all Creation. Although I'd had but a taste, I knew the experience was a profound gift that would help sustain me through whatever terrain lay before me in life. I would leave Alaska having been deeply blessed by her wild heart and spirit.

Our wilderness week was a true miracle. Southeastern Alaska receives over four feet of rain annually, much of it during the fall. The weeks leading up to our adventure had seen heavy wind and rains. Our chosen mode of entry and departure was by bush plane, so if the weather had not cleared, all our planning would have been for naught. As it turned out, we had a glorious week of autumn weather. On the afternoon of our departure, the curtains closed behind us. The rains and roaring winds returned. But I knew the gifts from Alaska would shine in my soul forever.

Epilogue

*T*o cope and heal from trauma, I had to change. I had to change my thoughts and limiting beliefs about myself. I had to learn new ways to get my needs met, to stay in my power, be in relationships, care for myself and so much more. Our mind, body and soul's natural design toward wholeness gives us a leg to stand on for such a transformational journey.

Honoring our authentic self is often a long road, given by not only our trauma history, but the cultural messages we are bombarded with relentlessly. So much of our self-image has been defined by outside forces. To tap into our own true identity, we need courage, determination, patience and self-love. Ideally, we'll have family, friends and healing teams who can support us on this journey back to ourselves.

To really become our whole self, we must have a spiritual life. We must tap into the ineffable source that is within us and all around us, through whatever practices resonate for us. I was drawn to the shamanic journey process as it allows immediate access to other realms of consciousness, offering direct spiritual assistance and healing. Time in nature remains a balm to my mind, body and soul and nourishes me like nothing else. I believe that our separation from nature and the violation of our wild animals and wild places has left a deep scar on the soul of humanity. Individually and collectively, we must find our way back to healing our relationship with the Earth and all Creation.

I have felt called to a Spirit led life, although this has compelled me to sometimes make difficult journeys into terrain I would have preferred to avoid. I've taken leap after leap into unknown territory at the beckoning of this "Spirit Call", sometimes to my delight, and sometimes to my dismay. Yet, there is no experience that does not serve us in some way, if we ask our own inner wisdom, "How is this experience serving me? What is it trying to teach me?"

An essential aspect of our healing journey, especially from trauma, is to repair and deepen our ability to trust ourselves, others, our circumstances and our own inner knowing. When embarking on a spiritual and healing journey, this becomes part of our "practice". We practice trust and become trusting. We practice being trustworthy, and we gain trust. The more we can trust ourselves, others and the universe, the more we can let go of control, and allow things to unfold in their own divine timing.

There's a delicate balance to being empowered while allowing our spiritual good, divine timing and universal laws to unfold in our lives. I've certainly known both experiences, and learned that forcing something into being can have a devastating outcome. Now, when faced with a major decision, I do lots of inner listening, rather than charging ahead on the first impulse. Life is a dance, and we must change our dance to keep time with the changing rhythms of our souls, hearts and our individual and collective journeys.

We've been culturally taught that life is a linear process. Who needs to be shackled by yet another set of limiting beliefs?! I now live life honoring its seasons and cycles of death and rebirth. There are seasons of growth and expansion, and seasons of going within, withdrawing; seasons of plenty and seasons of more limited resources. Nature's seasons and cycles remind us of this. And each of us has our own divine life line, our own destiny calling; and neither is bound to a linear clock and calendar.

Healing is a process and a journey. And no two individuals walk that path the same way. What is the way for one is not necessarily the way for another. For anyone who has experienced trauma, the journey can at times seem like we're treading water, or even losing ground. There are many layers and dimensions to healing and integrating these shifting energies. And every aspect of healing affects our whole being. As we address and heal one issue, it may cause another to surface, as it's no longer being held in place by the formerly unhealed part.

In the early stages of healing we may feel like we've opened a Pandora's Box of emotions. The journey can feel too intense, and we wish we could just climb back in the box and close the lid. But once we've said, "Yes!" to our healing process, it's hard to stop the train and get off. Our whole system seeks balance and wholeness, it longs for healing. We can ask for rests along the way; we can ask for gentle unfolding of our process, and we can seek out those healing arts and therapeutic practitioners we feel can best support us on our journey.

Blocked and stuffed emotions are a poison in our system; it's important to find safe and healthy ways to release them. So much can be cleared energetically from our chakras, energy field and soul. But we are emotional beings, and where there has been trauma, we will also find grief, anger, rage, fear and despair. Yet behind those dark clouds are healing, forgiveness, trust, joy, peace, wisdom and freedom.

There is one incredible core truth to healing. Any spiritual wound can be healed from the place of energy and Spirit. What is always behind that heavy energy of trauma is Unconditional Love. This is why the great spiritual masters speak of our world and our hurts as being but illusions. How can they be illusions when they hurt so much? Yes, these wounds hurt, and suffering is real for many millions on our planet right now. And yet, unconditional love is readily available, if we only could remember how to access it. When we work with intention to heal, LOVE is always present and available on the other side of trauma, just as the sun is always still shining behind the clouds on a stormy day.

Energy medicine and shamanic healing activate the wisdom and power of our soul, often hidden behind the shadow of trauma. I was able to heal incredibly painful and disabling wounds and reclaim soul essence lost many lifetimes ago. Through the window of soul and shamanic healing, I accessed powerful energies for healing myself and assisting others. Healing is an act of reclaiming our authentic powers and gifts. As we activate our soul's ability to heal, we restore more and more of the power we lost as a "victim". Activating our soul is a journey back to ourselves, to the core of our true power and wisdom; it is from this place we are most empowered to manifest our dreams.

We are really all on the same journey. We all come from Source and will return to Source, many times on our soul's journey. Our purpose is to love and be loved. The Seeds of Light are taking root in our individual and collective consciousness. With the assistance of the Ascended Masters of Light, Spiritual Lineages of Healers, Angelic Realms and our own personal helping spirit guides and healing teams, we have tremendous support during this time of the Great Awakening.

Many shamanic and energy healers around the world have prepared themselves to be of service to humanity and the Earth at this time in our spiritual evolution. And many more are stepping forward. If you seek personal healing, or feel called to service as a healer, trust your inner guidance and soul wisdom to align you with your path of healing and of service.

When we make the choice to heal our own lives, we help heal our families, our communities, our nation and the world. With every act of healing, we restore more Love and Light to ourselves and the Web of Creation. The love that comes to us through our healing is unconditional and eternal. It is the same love that accompanies the birth of every child, and the bloom of every flower. It is the love that shines from the stars, and sparkles in the eyes of a loved one. Each of us carries this spark of Universal Divine Light. And one day, when we step fully into our destiny as humans, we will light up the whole world with our Love.

We carry our human destiny in our DNA Codes and Rainbow Soul. When the Codes of Light have been fully activated across all continents and among all peoples in great enough numbers, the divisions which separate us nation from nation, race from race, religion from religion, gender from gender, will fall away. We will remember our place in the Web of Life, extending our Love and Light to All Creation. As foreseen by Black Elk and other great mystics, the Sacred Hoop, now broken, will be mended. The Sacred Tree of Life will flower in our hearts once more.   *- Debra LightHeart*

Note to the Reader

$\mathcal{A}$s a memoir, this book is largely based on experiences from my life, written as the story lives in me, and as it wanted to be expressed. While largely based on "facts", this memoir also partially relies on the oral histories that come down through families. As such, certain facts and truths get lost or embellished, or may not reflect the "truth" the way others see it. Yet, the only story I can tell, is the one I have lived and experienced, however flawed it might appear to another.

In a few instances, small events were combined for the sake of storytelling, and some names have been changed to honor privacy of individuals. I've attempted to be historically accurate, but this is not intended to be a book rooted in historical facts, but rather oral history and soul memory.

This story is not over. It lives on in the hearts, minds and souls of those who lived it and whose soul's journeys continue to unfold. This story lives on in the storyteller and the reader who have now woven their energies together through the sharing of this book. Where does the story go from here? Wherever our heart and soul lead us; if we are listening and willing to follow.

May our journeys be ever expansive and filled with great Beauty, Healing, Wisdom, Peace, Joy, Love and Light. And so it is.

Debra LightHeart
Santa Fe, NM
August, 2014

Resource List

The Foundation for Shamanic Studies, Founded by Michael Harner, Ph.D.
www.shamanism.org

The Four Winds Society, founded by Alberto Villoldo, Ph.D.
www.thefourwinds.com

www.Munay-Ki.org

American Polarity Therapy Association
www.polaritytherapy.org

Short List – Recommended Books

Shamanism/Shamanic Healing

Shaman, Healer, Sage *** *Mending the Past and Healing the Future* by Alberto Villoldo, Ph.D.

Soul Retrieval *** *Shamanic Journey, A Beginner's Guide* by Sandra Ingerman, MA

The Way of the Shaman **** *Cave and Cosmos* by Michael Harner, Ph.D

Recovery and Healing

Facing Co-Dependence by Pia Melody

Waking the Tiger **** *Trauma Proofing Your Kids* by Peter Levine, Ph.D.

Drama of the Gifted Child by Alice Miller, Ph.D.

Love, Medicine and Miracles by Bernie Siegel, MD

To See Differently, Personal Growth and Being of Service Through Attitudinal Healing by Susan Trout, Ph.D.

About the Author

*D*ebra LightHeart has been deeply drawn to nature, creative expression and matters of the soul and spirit since childhood. She first decided she would someday write a book about her life experiences when she was eight years old. After years of liberal arts studies, Debra graduated with a Bachelor of Science Degree from the University of New Hampshire. She pursued a rewarding career serving arts and social service organizations in the non-profit sector for some twenty five years.

As her own healing journey unfolded, Debra completed practitioner level trainings in energy medicine and shamanic healing and was initiated into the lineage of the Q'ero shamans of the Peruvian Andes. Debra has been offering healing sessions, workshops, ceremonies and retreats since 1996.

Extensions of her shamanic practice include writing, teaching, musical expression and creative arts. She has been writing personally and professionally since a young age; her first published essay was printed in the New Hampshire Audubon Journal when she was fifteen. Her art prints have sold internationally, and her *Star Gazer* bear painting was published in the 2011 *We'Moon* wall calendar.

Debra's passion is sharing the wisdom, power and beauty of the shamanic path with those who are seeking to heal and empower their lives, deepen their connection to Spirit and Nature, enhance expression of their creative gifts and fully manifest their dreams and life purpose. She is a New England native, and now lives with her aging dog and frisky cat in Santa Fe, New Mexico, nestled in the foothills of the Sangre de Cristo Mountains. She returns to New England often to be with family, friends and the sea.

Visit the Author on-line at www.debralightheart.com